EX LIBRIS

CLARKSON POTTER/PUBLISHERS

NEW YORK

EX·LIBRIS

MICHIKO KAKUTANI

ILLUSTRATED BY

DANA TANAMACHI

Library of Congress Cataloging-in-Publication Data
Names: Kakutani, Michiko, author.
Title: Ex Libris : 100+ Books to Read and Reread /
    Michiko Kakutani; illustrations by Dana Tanamachi.
Identifiers: LCCN 2020007615 (print) | LCCN 2020007616
    (ebook) | ISBN 9780525574972 (hardcover) | ISBN
    9780525574989 (ebook)
Subjects: LCSH: Best books. | Kakutani, Michiko—
    Books and reading. | Books and reading—United States.
Classification: LCC Z1035.9 .K35 2020 (print) | LCC Z1035.9
    (ebook) | DDC 028—dc23
LC record available at https://lccn.loc.gov/2020007615
LC ebook record available at https://lccn.loc.gov/2020007616

ISBN 978-0-525-57497-2
Ebook ISBN 978-0-525-57498-9

Printed in China

Book design by Danielle Deschenes
Cover illustrations by Dana Tanamachi

10 9 8 7 6 5 4 3 2 1

First Edition

FOR READERS AND WRITERS

EVERYWHERE

CONTENTS

➤➤➤ ✿ ⫷⫷

INTRODUCTION

As a child, the Pulitzer Prize–winning playwright August Wilson recalled in a speech that he was the one in his family who wanted to read all the books in the house, who wore out his library card and kept books way past their due date. He dropped out of high school at age fifteen, but spent every school day at the Carnegie Library of Pittsburgh reading history and biography and poetry and anthropology. The library would eventually give him an honorary high school diploma, and the books he discovered there, he said, "opened a world that I entered and have never left," and led to the transformative realization that "it was possible to be a writer."

Dr. Oliver Sacks credited the local public library he knew as a child (in Willesden, London) as the place where he received his real education, just as Ray Bradbury described himself as "completely library educated." In the case of two famous autodidacts, Abraham Lincoln and Frederick Douglass, the books they read growing up indelibly shaped their ideals and ambitions, and gave them the tools of language and argument that would help them shape the history of their nation.

The pleasure of reading, Virginia Woolf wrote, is "so great that one cannot doubt that without it the world would be a far different and a far inferior place from what it is. Reading has changed the world and continues to change it." In fact, she argued, the reason "we have grown from apes to men, and left our caves and dropped our bows and arrows and sat round the fire and talked and given to the poor and helped the sick—the reason why we have made shelter and society out of the wastes of the desert and the tangle of the jungle is simply this—we have loved reading."

In his 1996 book, *A History of Reading*, Alberto Manguel described a tenth-century Persian potentate who reportedly traveled with his 117,000-book collection loaded on the backs of "four hundred camels trained to walk in alphabetical order." Manguel also wrote about the public readers hired by Cuban cigar factories in the late nineteenth century to read aloud to workers. And about the father of one of his boyhood teachers, a scholar who knew many of the classics by heart and who volunteered to serve as a library for his fellow inmates at the Nazi concentration camp Sachsenhausen. He was able to recite entire passages aloud—much like the book lovers in *Fahrenheit 451*, who keep knowledge alive through their memorization of books.

Why do we love books so much?

These magical brick-sized objects—made of paper, ink, glue, thread, cardboard, fabric, or leather—are actually tiny time machines that can transport us back to the past to learn the lessons of history, and forward to idealized or dystopian futures. Books can transport us to distant parts of the globe and even more distant planets and universes. They give us the stories of men and women we will never meet in person, illuminate the discoveries made by great minds, and allow us access to the wisdom of earlier generations. They can teach us about astronomy, physics, botany, and chemistry; explicate the dynamics of space flight and climate change; introduce us to beliefs, ideas, and literatures different from our own. And they can whisk us off to fictional realms like Oz and Middle-earth, Narnia and Wonderland, and the place where Max becomes king of the wild things.

When I was a child, books were both an escape and a sanctuary. I was an only child, accustomed to spending lots of time alone. I read in the cardboard refrigerator carton that my father had turned into a playhouse by cutting a door and windows in the sides. I read under the blankets at night with a flashlight. I read in the school library during recess in hopes of avoiding the playground bullies. I read in the backseat of the car, even though it made me carsick. And I read at the dining room table: because my mother thought books and food were incompatible, I would read whatever happened to be at hand—cereal boxes, appliance manuals, supermarket circulars, the ingredients of Sara Lee's pecan coffee cake or an Entenmann's crumb cake. I read the recipe for mock apple pie on the back of the Ritz crackers box so many times I could practically recite it. I was hungry for words.

The characters in some novels felt so real to me, when I was a child, that I worried they might leap out of the pages at night, if I left the cover of the book open. I imagined some of the scary characters from L. Frank Baum's *Oz* books—the Winged Monkeys, say, or the evil Nome King, or Mombi the witch who possesses the dangerous Powder of Life—escaping from the books and using my bedroom as their portal into the real world, where they might wreak havoc and destruction.

Decades before binge-watching *Game of Thrones, Breaking Bad,* and *The Sopranos,* I binge-read Nancy Drew mysteries, *Black Stallion* novels, Landmark biographies, even whole sections of the *World Book Encyclopedia* (which is how my father fine-tuned his English, when he first moved to the United States from Japan).

In high school and college, I binge-read books about

existentialism (*The Stranger, No Exit, Notes from Underground, Irrational Man, Either/Or, The Birth of Tragedy*), black history (*The Autobiography of Malcolm X; The Fire Next Time; Manchild in the Promised Land; Black Like Me; Black Skin, White Masks*); and science fiction and dystopian fiction (*1984, Animal Farm, Dune, The Illustrated Man,* and *Fahrenheit 451, Childhood's End, A Clockwork Orange, Cat's Cradle*). My reading was in no way systematic. At the time, I was not even aware of why I gravitated toward these books—though, in retrospect, as one of the few nonwhite kids at school, I must have been drawn to books about outsiders who were trying to figure out who they were and where they belonged. Even Dorothy in Oz, Alice in Wonderland, and Lucy in Narnia, I later realized, were strangers in strange lands, trying to learn how to navigate worlds where few of the usual rules applied.

In those pre-internet days, I don't remember exactly how we heard about new books and authors or decided what to read next. As a child, I think I first heard of Hemingway, Robert Penn Warren, James Baldwin, and Philip Roth because there were articles by or about them (or maybe photos) in *Life* or *Look* magazine. I read Rachel Carson's *Silent Spring* because my mother was reading it, and T. S. Eliot's poetry because my favorite high school teacher, Mr. Adinolfi, had us memorize "The Love Song of J. Alfred Prufrock." I was one of those readers who experienced many things first through books—and only later, in real life, not the other way around.

"You read something which you thought only happened to you," James Baldwin once said, "and you discovered it happened 100 years ago to Dostoyevsky. This is a very great liberation for the suffering, struggling person, who always thinks that he is alone. This is why art is important."

The books I write about in these pages include some longtime favorites (*A Wrinkle in Time, Moby-Dick, The Palm at the End of the Mind*), some older books that illuminate our troubled politics today (*The Paranoid Style in American Politics, The Origins of Totalitarianism, The Federalist Papers*), some well-known works of fiction that have continued to exert a formative influence on successive generations of writers (*Winesburg, Ohio; As I Lay Dying; The Odyssey*), works of journalism and scholarship that address some of the most pressing issues of our day (*The Forever War, The Sixth Extinction, Dawn of the New Everything*), works that shine a light on hidden corners of our world or the human mind (*Arctic Dreams, Lab Girl, The Man Who Mistook His Wife for a Hat*), and books that I've frequently given or recommended to friends.

Some of my favorite classics are here, but there are lots of lists out there of must-read classics, not to mention the class syllabi we remember from high school and college. And so, I've also tried to include a lot of recent books—novels, stories, and memoirs by contemporary writers, and nonfiction works about how technology and political and cultural upheavals are bringing tectonic changes to our world.

Like all lists and anthologies, the selections here are subjective and decidedly arbitrary. It was difficult to whittle my choices down to a hundred (which is why some entries actually contain more than one book), and I could easily have added another hundred books that are equally powerful, moving, or timely.

Over the years, I had the good fortune to have some inspiring teachers who enriched my understanding and appreciation of books. And some wonderful editors—like *The New York Times*'s former managing editor Arthur Gelb, a mentor to many of us and a journalist equally at home in the world of culture and the world of breaking news—who made it possible for me to make a living for many years by reading.

In these pages, I'm writing less as a critic than as an enthusiast. I'm not trying to explicate hidden meanings in these books or situate them in a literary continuum; I'm trying to encourage you to read or reread these books, because they deserve as wide an audience as possible. Because they are affecting or timely or beautifully written. Because they teach us something about the world or other people or our own emotional lives. Or simply because they remind us why we fell in love with reading in the first place.

Today, in our contentious and fragmented world, reading matters more than ever. For one thing, books offer the sort of in-depth experience that's increasingly rare in our distracted, ADD age— be it the sense of magical immersion offered by a compelling novel, or the deep, meditative thinking triggered by a wise or provocative work of nonfiction.

Books can open a startling window on history; they can give us an all-access pass to knowledge both old and new. As the former defense secretary James Mattis, who assembled a seven-thousand-volume library, said of his years in the military, "Thanks to my reading, I have never been caught flat-footed by any situation, never at a loss for how any problem has been addressed before. It doesn't give me all the answers, but it lights what is often a dark path ahead."

Most of all, books can catalyze empathy—something more and more precious in our increasingly polarized and tribal world. Reading, Jean Rhys once wrote, "makes immigrants of us all. It takes us away from home, but more important, it finds homes for us everywhere."

Over the years, I had the good fortune to have some inspiring teachers who enriched my understanding and appreciation of books.

At its best, literature can surprise and move us, challenge our certainties, and goad us into reexamining our default settings. Books can jolt us out of old habits of mind and replace reflexive us-versus-them thinking with an appreciation of nuances and context. Literature challenges political orthodoxies, religious dogma, and conventional thinking (which, of course, is why authoritarian regimes ban and burn books), and it does what education and travel do: it exposes us to a multiplicity of viewpoints and voices.

Literature, as David Foster Wallace has pointed out, gives the reader, "marooned in her own skull," imaginative "access to other selves."

Or, as President Barack Obama observed during his last week in the White House, books can supply historical perspective, a sense of solidarity with others, and "the ability to get in somebody else's shoes." They can remind us of "the truths under the surface of what we argue about every day," and the capacity of "stories to unify—as opposed to divide, to engage rather than to marginalize."

In a world riven by political and social divisions, literature can connect people across time zones and zip codes, across cultures and religions, national boundaries and historical eras. It can give us an understanding of lives very different from our own, and a sense of the shared joys and losses of human experience.

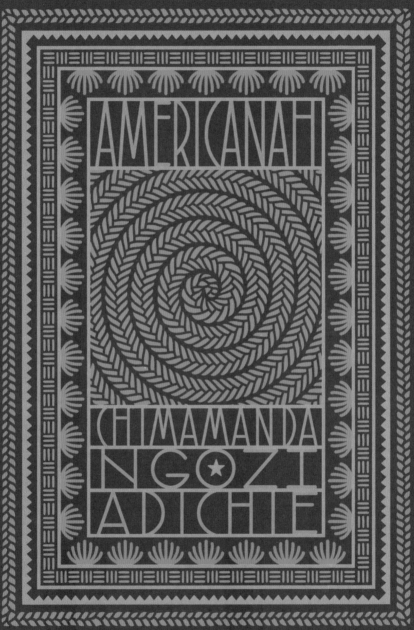

AMERICANAH

(2013)

Chimamanda Ngozi Adichie

With *Americanah*, Chimamanda Ngozi Adichie has written a wonderfully touching, incisive, and very funny coming-of-age tale that's both an old-fashioned love story and a sharp-eyed meditation on race, class, immigration, and identity in our rapidly changing, globalized world.

Adichie's spirited and outspoken heroine, Ifemelu, grows up in Lagos, Nigeria, where she falls in love, in high school, with Obinze, the earnest and quietly charming son of a literature professor. The two have instant chemistry—"she realized, quite suddenly, that she wanted to breathe the same air as Obinze"—and picture a future together, possibly in America, a country Obinze reveres.

When teacher strikes interrupt their college lives and Ifemelu receives a scholarship to attend university in America, Obinze urges her to take it. He tells her that he will get a visa and follow her there as soon as he completes his college degree, but harsh post-9/11 immigration policies will prevent this from happening. He will instead spend several miserable years as an illegal immigrant in London, where he is unable to find any but the most menial jobs. Eventually, he returns to Lagos, where he becomes a successful property developer, marries, and has a child.

Ifemelu, meanwhile, struggles to adapt to life in America. She compares what she sees firsthand with memories of *Cosby Show* episodes she watched growing up. And she hungers "to understand

Adichie has a heat-seeking eye for telling social and emotional details, and she uses that gift to convey Ifemelu's experiences with extraordinary immediacy.

everything about America"—"to support a team at the Super Bowl, understand what a Twinkie was and what sports 'lockouts' meant," order "a 'muffin' without thinking that it really was cake." Back home, she hadn't really thought of herself as "black," and she's startled by how ubiquitous arguments about race are in the United States, permeating everything from romances to friendships to on-the-job dynamics. In a blog post addressed to "Fellow Non-American Blacks," she writes, "Stop arguing. Stop saying I'm Jamaican or I'm Ghanaian. America doesn't care. So what if you weren't 'black' in your country? You're in America now."

Adichie has a heat-seeking eye for telling social and emotional details, and she uses that gift to convey Ifemelu's experiences with extraordinary immediacy while satirizing both the casual racism of some Americans and the sanctimony of those progressives eager to wear their liberal politics like a badge.

As a foreigner, Ifemelu notices the myriad oddities of American culture with wry humor. She notices that Americans tend to stand around and drink at parties, instead of dancing; that many "wear pajamas to school and underwear to the mall" to send the message that they are too "superior/busy/cool/not-uptight" to bother looking nice. She notices that they call arithmetic "math," not "maths," and that academic types can get bizarrely incensed over matters like "imported vegetables that ripened in trucks."

As the years scroll by, Ifemelu achieves success with her blog called *Raceteenth or Curious Observations by a Non-American Black on the Subject of Blackness in America.* She is confident in a way she hadn't been before, and after a breakup with a wealthy white businessman she settles into a perfect-on-paper relationship with a black professor who teaches at Yale.

But Ifemelu cannot stop thinking about Obinze, "her first love, her first lover, the only person with whom she had never felt the need to explain herself." And she realizes that "the cement in her soul" that she often feels is a kind of homesickness—for Lagos and her family. And so, after thirteen years, she decides to return home—a journey that proves as jarring as her voyage to America. Her experiences, so powerfully recounted by Adichie, become a story about belonging and not-belonging in a world where identities are both increasingly fluid and defining, a story about how we are shaped by the places where we grew up and the places where we come to live.

THE LIGHT OF THE WORLD
A Memoir

(2015)

Elizabeth Alexander

In this haunting memoir about love and loss and grief, Elizabeth Alexander describes the shattering emotional aftermath of the death of her beloved husband, Ficre Ghebreyesus, and how she and her two sons, Solomon and Simon, consoled one another and guided one another through a dark corridor of sorrow and back out into the light.

One night at bedtime, she recalls, thirteen-year-old Simon asks her if she wants to come with him to visit Ficre in heaven:

"Yes, I say, and lie down on his bed.

"'First you close your eyes,' he says, 'and ride the clear glass elevator. Up we go.'

"What do you see? I ask.

"God is sitting at the gate, he answers.

"What does God look like? I ask.

"Like God, he says. Now, we go to where Daddy is.

"He has two rooms, Simon says, one room with a single bed and his books and another where he paints. The painting room is vast. He can look out any window he wants and paint."

When it's time to leave, they take the elevator back down. "You can come with me anytime," Simon tells his mother.

Alexander—an award-winning poet and a former professor at Yale University who is currently president of the Andrew W. Mellon Foundation—communicates the raw grief she experienced in losing her husband of fifteen years. Her book is really a love letter to him, and it leaves us with an indelible portrait of Ghebreyesus as husband, father, and artist. She brings his brilliantly colored paintings alive on the page. She describes how they met. And she remembers how they fell in love, cooking together, writing haikus to each other in a shared notebook, listening to Ahmad Jamal, Betty Carter, Abbey Lincoln, Randy Weston, and Don Pullen, "geniuses of the African diaspora we both celebrated."

Just as her poetry (*American Sublime, The Venus Hottentot, Antebellum Dream Book*) explores the connections between the present and the past and the complexities of identity, so this memoir memorializes the strange twists of fate that can bring two people together. Alexander and Ghebreyesus, it turns out, were born within two months of each other, on opposite sides of the globe—she in Harlem; he in war-torn Eritrea, which he fled at the age of sixteen, making his way to America by way of Sudan, Italy, and Germany.

In the wake of his death, Alexander feels their house suffused in sorrow. She feels she "can wait forever for him to come back"; she will "leave the light on in the living room, the light that faces the street." She dreams of his returning, improbably, on a skateboard. She thinks, "I am getting older and he is not."

She realizes she does not know how to operate the DVR because it made no sense for both of them to learn how. She continues to pay his cell phone bill for a year and a half afterward, because she didn't want to lose the text messages. She avoids bookstores because she imagines seeing him in the history section or the art section or the gardening section.

Alexander and Ghebreyesus met in New Haven and raised their two boys there and in nearby Hamden. Writing as both a poet and a longtime resident, she perfectly captures New Haven's "mixed-metaphor landscape of New England trees and industrial detritus," as well as its unexpectedly excellent food and the mixed rhythms of college life and street life.

Alexander's book ends with her and her sons leaving New Haven for New York. They plan to stop by Grove Street Cemetery to say goodbye to Ficre, but they are delayed by a doctor's appointment and don't make it to the cemetery before closing time. It's okay, her son Simon says: "The grave reminds me of Daddy's death, but I want to remember Daddy's life."

Just as her poetry explores the connections between the present and the past and the complexities of identity, so this memoir memorializes the strange twists of fate that can bring two people together.

MUHAMMAD ALI

THE GREATEST: My Own Story (1975)
Muhammad Ali (with Richard Durham)

THE MUHAMMAD ALI READER (1998)
Edited by Gerald Early

*KING OF THE WORLD: Muhammad Ali and the
Rise of an American Hero* (1998)
David Remnick

THE TRIBUTE: Muhammad Ali, 1942–2016 (2016)
Sports Illustrated

He said it best, of course: He was "the astronaut of boxing" who "handcuffed lightning," threw "thunder in jail"; the dazzling warrior "with iron fists and a beautiful tan"; "the greatest fighter that ever will be" who could "run through a hurricane" and not get wet.

Muhammad Ali not only rocked the world with his electrifying speed and power in the ring. He also shook the world with the force of his convictions: his determination to stand up to the racist rules of the Jim Crow South and to assert his freedom to invent himself—"I don't have to be what you want me to be. I'm free to be what I want."

"I am America," he proudly declared, decades before the Black Lives Matter movement. "I am the part you won't recognize. But get used to me. Black, confident, cocky; my name, not yours; my religion, not yours; my goals, my own; get used to me." He stood with Martin Luther King, Jr., for freedom and social justice. And he stood up against the Vietnam War, refusing to be drafted in 1967 on religious grounds as a conscientious objector—a decision that would cost him his boxing title, three and a half years of his career at the peak of his powers, tens of millions of dollars in prize money and endorsements, and for many years his popularity.

Ali was a larger-than-life figure: not just an incandescent athlete dancing under the lights, but a man of conscience who spoke truth to power, as well as a captivating showman, poet, philosopher, performance artist, statesman, and hip-hop pioneer, a man compared to Whitman, Robeson, Malcolm X, Ellington, and Chaplin. Writers were magnetized by his contradictions: the GOAT (Greatest of All Time), who vanquished some of the baddest men on the planet but became one of the world's most revered humanitarians; a deeply religious man who loved practical jokes and practically invented trash talk; "a radical even in a radical's time," as President Obama put it, who became so beloved by Americans across the political spectrum that he was featured in a DC Comics book in which he teamed up with Superman to save the world.

Over the years, Ali has also inspired an uncommon amount of arresting writing, from Norman Mailer's classic account of the boxer's stunning victory over George Foreman in Zaire in 1974 to David Remnick's *King of the World,* a powerful account of Ali's emergence as a transformative figure in American politics and culture. There is also a plethora of memorable essays about Ali by such gifted writers as Joyce Carol Oates, George Plimpton, Tom Wolfe, Hunter S. Thompson, and Roger Kahn, many of which can be found in a terrific anthology, *The Muhammad Ali Reader.*

As for iconic photographs of Ali, many appear in *Sports Illustrated*'s *Muhammad Ali, 1942–2016.* They are photos that capture what the fighter José Torres called "his prodigious magic":

the famous photo of a victorious Ali, standing over the fallen body of Sonny Liston; a violent action shot of him catching George Foreman with a hard right in the Rumble in the Jungle; and one of him locked in a grim face-off with an exhausted Joe Frazier in the Thrilla in Manila. There are also images of a skinny, twelve-year-old Cassius Clay learning to box, and a solemn Ali, surrounded by reporters, explaining his opposition to the Vietnam War.

These books remind us that perseverance was one of the consistent themes in Ali's life: coming back after his government-imposed exile to reclaim the world championship in 1974 by toughing it out against Foreman in Zaire; coming back to beat Frazier twice, after losing their first arduous matchup; and coming back against Leon Spinks in 1978 to win the world heavyweight championship for a third time. As Ali once observed, "Champions aren't made in gyms. Champions are made from something they have deep inside them—a desire, a dream, a vision . . . the will must be stronger than the skill."

When Cassius Clay was growing up in Louisville, Kentucky, the town was segregated, and even when he returned home from the 1960 Olympics with a gold medal around his neck, he was turned away from a luncheonette. He would return to the Olympics three and a half decades later in Atlanta in 1996 as its final torchbearer; by then, he'd become one of the most revered human beings on the planet.

Ali died on June 3, 2016, and as his funeral motorcade made its way through the city, mourners showered his car with flowers and rose petals. All along the route, the Louisville *Courier-Journal* reported, lawns had been mowed and driveways freshly swept—out of respect for the Greatest on his final journey.

EXPERIENCE
A Memoir

(2000)

Martin Amis

W hat is it like to grow up aspiring to become a novelist, when your father is himself a well-known novelist? Martin Amis's 2000 memoir, *Experience,* addresses that question with great humor and affection, and creates a moving portrait of a father-son relationship animated by clear-eyed literary insight, enduring love, and a novelist's ability to animate the past with remarkable emotional detail.

The literary kinship between Martin Amis and his father, Kingsley, has long been clear to fans of both writers' work. Both got their start as angry young men with a dyspeptic gift for satire and biting humor. Both wrote classic novels featuring feckless, self-deluded heroes (Jim Dixon in Amis père's *Lucky Jim,* and John Self and Richard Tull in Amis fils's *Money* and *The Information*). And both fluently lived up to Amis senior's credo that "any proper writer ought to be able to write anything from an Easter Day sermon to a sheep-dip handout."

Over the years, Martin Amis's books leapfrogged over his father's in terms of innovation and ambition. *London Fields* (1989) was a dark satire set in a decadent, apocalyptic world, while the powerful *House of Meetings* (2006) addressed the daunting subject of the Soviet gulag. If such novels spoke to his willingness to tackle huge, historical subjects and experiment with voice and genre and technique, *Experience* brought a new warmth and depth of emotion to his writing.

It could not have been easy being Kingsley Amis's son. The elder Amis's acidic memoirs, published in 1991, not only settled dozens of literary scores but also drew a self-portrait of a prickly and unsparing curmudgeon. Kingsley Amis gave interviews characterizing his son's books as unreadable, his politics as "dangerous, howling nonsense."

EXPERIENCE *creates a moving portrait of a father-son relationship animated by clear-eyed literary insight, enduring love, and a novelist's ability to animate the past with remarkable emotional detail.*

"My father never encouraged me to write, never invited me to go for that longshot," Martin Amis writes in *Experience*, "he praised me less often than he publicly dispraised me."

The younger Amis suggests that some of his father's more provocative political statements were simply exercises in "winding me up," and in *Experience* he conveys the bantering, comradely quality of the relationship between his own younger self—"a drawling, velvet-suited, snakeskin-booted" adolescent cultivating a ridiculous "plumed and crested manner"—and Kingsley in his prime, a tireless womanizer, drinker, and raconteur, an inexhaustible "engine of comedy" within his own household.

Years later, Martin would take his two young sons to lunch at his father's almost every Sunday, and also joined his father for a garrulous midweek meal. When he left his wife for another woman in 1993, it was his father he turned to for solace and advice. "Only to him," he writes, "could I confess how terrible I felt, how physically terrible, bemused, subnormalized, stupefied from within, and always about to flinch or tremble from the effort of making my face look honest, kind, sane. Only to him could I talk about what I was doing to my children. Because he had done it to me."

Kingsley had long suffered from nyctophobia (fear of the night) and monophobia (fear of being alone), and in the wake of the collapse of his marriage to Elizabeth Jane Howard (for whom he had left Martin's mother) Martin and his brother began to take turns "Dadsitting," promising him that he'd never have to spend an evening alone.

In *Experience,* Martin Amis writes persuasively about a lot of things—literary friendships and disputes, the disappearance and murder of a beloved cousin, the horrors of dental surgery. But what's most indelible about this book is his writing—"for once, without artifice"—of the "ordinary miracles and ordinary disasters" of daily life, of what it means to be a son, and of what it means to be a father with children of his own.

WINESBURG, OHIO

(1919)

Sherwood Anderson

I t's hard to think of an American work of fiction that's been more influential than *Winesburg, Ohio,* Sherwood Anderson's 1919 volume of interlinked stories about the lonely residents of a small, fictional midwestern village.

Faulkner, Fitzgerald, and Steinbeck all paid tribute to Sherwood Anderson. Works as disparate as Faulkner's *Go Down, Moses,* Hemingway's *In Our Time,* Ray Bradbury's *Illustrated Man,* and Tim O'Brien's *The Things They Carried* would work variations on its innovative structure, while the fiction of Carson McCullers and Flannery O'Connor would be populated with outcasts and eccentrics reminiscent of the lost, the lonely, and the dispossessed in *Winesburg.* You can also count George Saunders, Raymond Carver, Denis Johnson, Russell Banks, and Tom Perrotta among the many contemporary writers who have written stories or novels that owe a direct or indirect debt to Anderson's classic.

Like Joyce's *Dubliners* (1914), the stories in *Winesburg* all take place in the same town, and they draw portraits of ordinary people whose ambitions have gone unrealized, whose dreams are receding in the rearview mirror. *Winesburg* depicts a small-town world where the sense of isolation people feel in their day-to-day lives reflects some of the larger dynamics at work in early twentieth-century America. It anticipates a changing social landscape in which more and more young people are leaving small towns for big cities and their suburbs, and the rural-urban divide is growing ever wider.

Anderson's stories share the twilight mood of Edward Hopper's paintings, and they similarly depict solitary individuals whose lives seem defined by missed connections and forfeited opportunities. Among the more than two dozen characters in the book, there's Doctor Reefy, an aging doctor and widower, who scribbles his thoughts on little pieces of paper that he puts in his pocket and eventually throws away; a lonely young woman named Alice who's unable to get over a boyfriend who moved on and moved away; Wash Williams, the telegraph operator, who hates life "wholeheartedly, with the abandon of a poet"; the Reverend Curtis Hartman, a minister who spies on a pretty woman through his window and asks for deliverance from temptation; Kate Swift, the schoolteacher, whom the minister lusts after and who encourages the literary aspirations of the book's young hero, George Willard; and George's mother, Elizabeth, the ailing proprietor of a shabby hotel, who has invested all her hopes and dreams in her son.

The story of George's coming of age provides the through line in these stories. A reporter for the local paper, he is the person many of the other characters confide in, and he becomes both a conduit for their stories and a kind of surrogate for Anderson, who himself grew up in a small Ohio town.

After his mother dies, George decides he is going to "leave Winesburg to go away to some city where he hoped to get work on a city newspaper." He does not want to become trapped in Winesburg like so many of the people he knows; he does not want "the spark of genius" his teacher saw in him to be extinguished. Like many bildungsromans, the book ends with the hero's departure from his hometown as he boards a train headed west—presumably to Chicago—"to meet the adventure of life."

THE ORIGINS OF TOTALITARIANISM

(1951)

Hannah Arendt

As Hannah Arendt observed in her 1951 book, *The Origins of Totalitarianism*, two of the most monstrous regimes in human history came to power in the twentieth century, and both were predicated upon the destruction of truth—upon the recognition that cynicism and weariness and fear can make people susceptible to the lies and false promises of leaders bent on unconditional power. "The ideal subject of totalitarian rule," she wrote, "is not the convinced Nazi or the convinced Communist, but people for whom the distinction between fact and fiction (*i.e.,* the reality of experience) and the distinction between true and false (*i.e.,* the standards of thought) no longer exist."

What's alarming to the contemporary reader is that Arendt's words increasingly sound less like a dispatch from another century than a disturbing mirror of the political and cultural landscape we inhabit today—a world in which the president of the United States, Donald J. Trump, does a high-volume business in lies (three years into his White House tenure, *The Washington Post* calculated, Trump had made 16,241 false or misleading claims), and fake news and propaganda are cranked out in industrial quantities by Russian and alt-right trolls and instantaneously dispersed across the world through social media.

Nationalism, nativism, dislocation, fears of social change, and contempt for outsiders are on the rise again as people, locked in their partisan silos and filter bubbles, are losing a sense of shared reality and the ability to communicate across social and sectarian lines.

This is not to draw a direct analogy between today's circumstances and the overwhelming horrors of the World War II era but to look at some of the conditions and attitudes—what Margaret Atwood has called the "danger flags" in Orwell's *1984* and *Animal Farm*—that make a people susceptible to demagogues and dictators, and nations vulnerable to tyranny.

Here are some of the fundamental points Arendt made about the "hidden mechanisms" by which totalitarian movements dissolve traditional political and moral understandings, and the behavior evinced by totalitarian regimes, once they come to power.

- One early warning sign is a nation's abolishing of the right of asylum. Efforts to deprive refugees of their rights, Arendt wrote, bear "the germs of a deadly sickness," because once the "principle of equality before the law" breaks down, "the more difficult it is for states to resist the temptation to deprive all citizens of legal status."

- Leaders of totalitarian movements, Arendt observed, "can never admit an error," and fanatical followers, suffering from a mixture of gullibility and cynicism, will routinely shrug off their lies. Hungry for simplistic narratives that explain a confusing world, such audiences "do not trust their eyes and ears" but, instead, welcome the "escape from reality" offered by propaganda, which understands that people are "ready at all times to believe the worst, no matter how absurd, and did not particularly object to being deceived," because they "held every statement to be a lie anyhow."

- Because totalitarian rulers crave complete control, Arendt pointed out, they tend to preside over highly dysfunctional bureaucracies. First-rate talents are replaced by "crackpots and fools whose lack of intelligence and creativity is still the best guarantee of their loyalty." Often there are "swift and surprising changes in policy" because loyalty—not performance or efficacy—is paramount.

- To ratify followers' sense of belonging to a movement that is making progress toward a distant goal, Arendt added, new opponents or enemies are repeatedly invoked; "as soon as one category is liquidated, war may be declared on another."

- Another trait of totalitarian governments, Arendt observed, is a perverse disdain for both "common sense and self-interest": a stance fueled by mendacity and denial of facts and embraced by megalomaniacal leaders, eager to believe that failures can be denied or erased and "mad enough to discard all limited and local interests—economic, national, human, military—in favor of a purely fictitious reality" that endows them with infallibility and absolute power.

The Origins of Totalitarianism is essential reading not only because it reminds us of the monstrous crimes committed by Nazi Germany and Stalin's Soviet Union in the twentieth century but also because it provides a chilling warning of the dynamics that could fuel totalitarian movements in the future. The book underscores how alienation, rootlessness, and economic uncertainty can make people susceptible to the lies and conspiracy theories dispensed by tyrants. It shows how the weaponization of bigotry and racism by demagogues fuels populist movements built upon tribal hatreds while undermining the long-standing institutions meant to protect our freedoms and the rule of law and shattering the very idea of a shared sense of humanity.

Margaret Atwood

The Handmaid's Tale

THE HANDMAID'S TALE

(1985)

Margaret Atwood

Enduring dystopian novels look backward and forward at the same time. Orwell's *1984* was, at once, a savage satire of Stalin's U.S.S.R. and a timeless anatomy of tyranny that foretold the rise of the surveillance state and the "firehose of falsehood" spewed forth daily by Putin's Kremlin and Trump's White House in efforts to redefine reality. Aldous Huxley's *Brave New World* reflected its author's worries in the 1930s that individual freedom was threatened by both communism and assembly-line capitalism, and it anticipated a technology-driven future in which people would be narcotized and distracted to death by trivia and entertainment.

In writing her 1985 classic, *The Handmaid's Tale,* Margaret Atwood decided she would include nothing in the novel "that had not already happened" somewhere, sometime in history, or any technology "not already available." She extrapolated some of the trends she saw in the 1970s and early 1980s (like the rising fundamentalist movement in America), looked back at the seventeenth-century Puritans' anti-women bias, and drew upon such historical horrors as the Nazis' *Lebensborn* program and public executions in countries like North Korea and Saudi Arabia to delineate the malign machinery of Gilead, the dystopian regime she imagined taking over the United States in some not-so-distant future.

When many of us first read *The Handmaid's Tale* back in the 1980s, the events Atwood described as taking place in Gilead felt like the sort of alarming developments that could only happen in the distant past or in distant parts of the globe. By 2019, however, American news reports were filled with real-life images of children being torn from their parents' arms, a president using racist language to sow fear and hatred, and reports of accelerating climate change threatening life as we know it on the planet.

How did the United States with its democratic norms and constitutional guarantees metamorphose, in *The Handmaid's Tale,* into the authoritarian state of Gilead—a place where women are treated as "two-legged wombs"; where nonwhite residents and unbelievers (that is, Jews, Catholics, Quakers, Baptists, anyone who does not embrace the fundamentalist extremism of Gilead) are resettled, exiled, or disappeared; where the leadership deliberately uses gender, race, and class to divide the country? It started before ordinary citizens like herself were paying attention, Atwood's heroine, Offred, remembers: "We lived, as usual, by ignoring. Ignoring isn't the same as ignorance, you have to work at it.

"Nothing changes instantaneously," she goes on. "In a gradually heating bathtub you'd be boiled to death before you knew it."

In fact, the most chilling lines in *The Handmaid's Tale* occur near the beginning of the novel. Offred and her shopping partner Ofglen are walking past the Wall—a landmark that once belonged to a famous university in Cambridge, Massachusetts, and that is now used by the rulers of Gilead to display the corpses of people executed as traitors. As she looks at six new bodies hanging there, Offred remembers the unnerving words of their warden Aunt Lydia: "ordinary," she said, is "what you are used to. This may not seem ordinary to you now, but after a time it will. It will become ordinary."

Atwood's Offred was not the ass-kicking leader of the resistance seen in seasons 2 and 3 of the Hulu television adaptation; she was not a rebel like her friend Moira and not an ideological feminist like her mother. If some readers found this Offred overly passive, her very ordinariness gave us an immediate understanding of how Gilead's tyrannical rule affected regular people's lives.

In a 2017 essay, Atwood described writing Offred's story in the tradition of "the literature of witness"—referring to those accounts left by people bearing witness to the calamities of history they've experienced firsthand: wars, atrocities, disasters, social upheavals, hinge moments in civilization. It's a genre that includes the diary of Anne Frank, the writings of Primo Levi, the choral histories assembled by the Nobel Prize winner Svetlana Alexievich from intensive interviews with Russians, remembering their daily lives during World War II, the Chernobyl accident, or the Afghanistan war. Agency and strength, Atwood seemed to be suggesting, do not require a heroine with the visionary gifts of Joan of Arc or the ninja skills of a Katniss Everdeen or Lisbeth Salander; there are other ways of defying tyranny, participating in the Resistance, or helping ensure the truth of the historical record.

The very act of writing or recording one's experiences, Atwood argued, is "an act of hope." Like messages placed in bottles tossed into the sea, witness testimonies count on someone, somewhere, being there to read their words—even if it's the pompous, myopic Gileadean scholars who narrate the satiric epilogues to *The Handmaid's Tale* and its 2019 sequel, *The Testaments.*

As Atwood no doubt knows, one of the definitions given by Bible dictionaries for "Gilead" is "hill of testimony." And in testifying to what she has witnessed, Offred left behind an account that challenged official Gileadean narratives, and in doing so, she was standing up to the regime's efforts to silence women by telling her own story in her own voice.

COLLECTED POEMS

W. H. Auden

→ →→ ✿ ←← ←

In the days after the 9/11 terrorist attacks, copies of W. H. Auden's poem "September 1, 1939" went viral by email and fax. The poem—which had originally been written in response to Hitler's invasion of Poland and the start of World War II in Europe—was reprinted in newspapers, read on National Public Radio, and discussed online. After Donald Trump won the 2016 election and after his inauguration the following January, Auden's poem was again widely shared and debated.

Auden, himself, had renounced the poem—and other early works that he had come to regard as glib or gauche or a vestige of his leftist youth. But the poem continues to resonate with readers because of its evocation of a dangerous moment in history. Auden writes of "waves of anger and fear" washing over the "darkened lands of the earth." He writes of humanity's tragic inability to learn from history—"the enlightenment driven away"—and how we seem fated to suffer "mismanagement and grief" over and over again. At the same time, echoing Matthew Arnold in "Dover Beach," Auden also looks for hope in the possibility of human connection and the urge to "show an affirming flame" in a world beleaguered by "negation and despair."

Auden's poems from the 1930s are concerned with the intersection of the public and the personal, and they also attest to his gifts as a kind of anthropologist—observing the worries and fears of people as the world headed off a cliff. The specter of fascism and the social ravages of the Great Depression rumble through many of these poems, which reverberate with apocalyptic premonitions, reminiscent of Yeats's "The Second Coming" (another widely shared poem on social media in the second decade of the millennium).

In his 1935 poem "To a Writer on His Birthday," Auden writes of the wireless roaring "its warnings and its lies" and notes that even people in pretty seaside towns will soon be swept along "on the dangerous flood / Of history that never sleeps or dies." In "Musée des Beaux Arts," written shortly after the Munich Pact was signed in 1938, Auden wrote about how easy it is to turn away from other people's suffering, how easily daily life can distract from catastrophe.

Auden moved to America in 1939, and his verse would grow increasingly focused on spiritual and emotional concerns. Though he contended that "poetry makes nothing happen," his own verse would continue to bear witness to the "age of anxiety," testifying to the possibilities and solace of art, even at a time when a nation feels "sequestered in its hate," and "Intellectual disgrace/ stares from every human face, / And the seas of pity lie / Locked and frozen in each eye."

CONTINENTAL DRIFT

(1985)

Russell Banks

Although Russell Banks's epic novel *Continental Drift* was published back in 1985, it tells "an American story" that feels uncommonly current in the opening of the third decade of the twenty-first century. The novel reminds us of the power of the old American dream—namely, the possibility of beginning a new life in the New World, of reinventing oneself, tabula rasa. And it anticipates the growing tensions between refugees desperate to reach American shores to escape violence and despair at home and those working-class Americans who have found their own hopes of economic security and a brighter future for their children slipping out of reach.

The novel's two central characters, Bob and Vanise, whose lives will violently collide, actually have a lot in common: both are disenfranchised and desperate, and determined to gamble everything on the chance of a better future.

Like many of Banks's protagonists, Bob Dubois hails from a small New England working-class town; Banks describes him as "an ordinary man, a decent man, a common man." At the age of thirty, he owns a run-down duplex, a thirteen-foot Boston whaler he built from a kit, and a battered Chevrolet station wagon. He owes the local savings and loan a little over twenty-two thousand dollars—for the house, the boat, and the car. "We have a good life," his wife, Elaine, insists, but Bob feels increasingly frustrated and trapped; "nothing seems improved over yesterday," and he's begun to worry that he will never achieve even his most modest dreams.

One day, he abruptly moves his family to Florida, where he soon finds himself in business with his wheeler-dealer brother, Eddie, and with Avery, a disreputable childhood pal who's been running drugs. For Banks's characters, Florida is what California was for people in books by Nathanael West and Raymond Chandler—a ragged, dangerous place where people play loose and fast with the rules, a magnet for dreamers, hustlers, con men, and people with no place else to go. Here, the old pioneer spirit has devolved into a kind of me-first individualism, and nerve and hubris and good luck can make you rich. Bob, however, is caught in a downward spiral—living in a trailer park and bereft even of the job and house that had lent his life in New Hampshire a modicum of stability.

Desperate for money, Bob agrees to help ferry some Haitian refugees from the Bahamas to Miami, and his life is set on a collision course with that of a young Haitian woman named Vanise who's set off for America with her infant child and a nephew, after their house was destroyed by a hurricane. She imagines that "everything will be different" in America, but instead she is cruelly abused by smugglers.

Banks not only gives the dovetailing stories of Vanise and Bob a terrible inevitability but also turns them into a dark story of our times.

BOOKS BY SAUL BELLOW

THE ADVENTURES OF AUGIE MARCH (1953)

HERZOG (1964)

THE ACTUAL: A Novella (1997)

S aul Bellow's most memorable novels are portraits of individuals trying to figure out their place in the world, what it means, as he wrote in *Herzog*, "to be a man. In a city. In a century. In transition. In a mass. Transformed by science. Under organized power. Subject to tremendous controls. In a condition caused by mechanization. After the late failure of radical hopes."

Though Bellow's heroes live mainly in the mid- to late twentieth century, their existential predicaments could not feel more timely today. Stuck in an American reality filled with calamities, con games, and cheap distractions, they struggle to find a balance between immersion in this "moronic inferno" and the more pristine realm of the self. Some of his "dangling men" suspect that all the "human nonsense" of daily life, from politics to business to romance, impedes their apprehension of the larger truths of the cosmos—"the axial lines" of "truth, love, peace, bounty, usefulness, harmony." But others are aware of the temptations of narcissism and isolation. Harry Trellman in *The Actual,* for instance, realizes that his judgmental intellect and craving for a higher life are the very things that have cut him off from humanity—and from love.

Readers all have their favorite Bellow novels. To me, the three that are marvels of storytelling and that most clearly embody his quintessential themes are *The Adventures of Augie March,* the 1953 picaresque novel that marked Bellow's discovery of an exuberant voice that was all his own; *Herzog,* a remarkable portrait of one man's midlife crisis and the human quest for meaning in an increasingly atomized age in which the old certainties of religion and ideology no longer hold; and *The Actual,* a late, elegiac, and very Jamesian tale about one man's belated efforts to step out of his lifelong role as an observer and submerge himself in (or at least dip a toe into) reality.

Bellow's heroes are first-class "noticers" who often feel overwhelmed by the "muchness" of the world and who wonder if their personal woes somehow hold a tiny mirror to the "big-scale insanities of the twentieth century." They are overly aware of mortality, the Big Clock, constantly ticking away in the distance.

Writing in prose that shifts gears effortlessly between the ebullient and the depressive, Bellow vividly conjured the busy mental life of his heroes—men who live, quite willfully, in their heads—and their daily, creaturely existence, as well as their encounters with what he called "reality instructors": assorted salesmen, con men, and fixers who goad his protagonists into a recognition of everyday life. In fact, Bellow's novels attest to his ease in grappling with big, Russian-novel-like ideas while at the same time using his gift for streetwise portraiture and description to capture the "daily monkeyshines" of "the cheapies, the stingies, the hypochondriacs, the family bores, humanoids," and barstool comedians who populate his hectic and captivating world.

THE IMAGE
A Guide to Pseudo-Events in America

(1962)

Daniel J. Boorstin

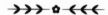

Published in 1962, Daniel J. Boorstin's book *The Image: A Guide to Pseudo-Events in America* uncannily foresaw the reality-show world we inhabit in the Trump era. For that matter, the book anticipated the arrival of someone very much like Donald J. Trump himself: a celebrity known, in Boorstin's words, for his "well-knownness," a loudmouthed showman, skilled in little besides self-promotion and staging what Boorstin called "pseudo-events"—that is, contrived events meant to generate publicity and appeal to the hunger of audiences for spectacle and diversion.

Boorstin's descriptions of the nineteenth-century impresario and circus showman P. T. Barnum—who ran a New York City museum of curiosities filled with hoaxes like a mermaid (which turned out to be the remains of a monkey stitched together with the tail of a fish)—will sound strangely familiar to contemporary readers: a self-proclaimed "prince of humbugs" whose "great discovery was not how easy it was to deceive the public but rather how much the public enjoyed being deceived" as long as it was being entertained.

In recounting how illusions were displacing knowledge, how advertising was taking the place of content, The Image would influence the work of myriad writers from French theorists like Baudrillard and Guy Debord to social critics like Neil Postman and Douglas Rushkoff. Decades before the rise of the internet, Boorstin envisaged the "thicket of unreality" that would increasingly come to surround us as fake news, conspiracy theories, and political propaganda proliferated over the World Wide Web.

Much the way that images were supplanting ideals, Boorstin wrote, the idea of "credibility" was replacing the idea of truth. People were less interested in whether something was a fact than in whether it was "convenient that it should be believed." And as verisimilitude increasingly replaced truth as a measurement, "the socially rewarded art" became "that of making things seem true." No surprise then that the new masters of the universe in the early 1960s were the Mad Men of Madison Avenue. No surprise that the Republican strategist Lee Atwater, anticipating the age of Trump, would argue in the 1980s that "perception is reality" and his clients—and many GOP supporters—would buy it.

Decades before the rise of the internet, Boorstin envisaged the "thicket of unreality" that would increasingly come to surround us as fake news, conspiracy theories, and political propaganda proliferated over the World Wide Web.

FICCIONES

(1944; English translation, 1962)

Jorge Luis Borges
Edited by Anthony Kerrigan
Translated by Alastair Reid, Anthony Kerrigan, Anthony Bonner, Helen
Temple, and Ruthven Todd

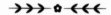

J orge Luis Borges's magical tales are like M. C. Escher drawings—
fascinating, enigmatic tableaux filled with labyrinths, mirrors,
and mazes that reverberate with a sense of metaphysical
mystery. The lines between the real and the imaginary blur together
here, as do the lines between writer and reader, life and art.

Translated into English in 1962, Borges's *Ficciones* presaged
many of the postmodernist techniques that would be embraced
by later generations of writers across the world. Some of his tales
reinvented familiar genres like the detective story, turning them
into philosophical meditations about time and the nature of cause
and effect. Some gave us fantastical events and strange beings:
transparent tigers, wizards who conjure up visions in a bowl of ink,
an encyclopedia that chronicles imaginary worlds. Some seemed
to foretell the dizzying world of the internet where we would be
deluged with tidal waves of data and multiplying, multifarious
possibilities.

"The Garden of Forking Paths" describes a novel that is a kind
of hypertext—filled with forking paths and alternate futures that
exist simultaneously. And "The Library of Babel" depicts the
universe as an infinite library, containing all knowledge past and

FICCIONES

JORGE LUIS BORGES

present. "Everything is there: the minute history of the future, the autobiographies of the archangels, . . . the veridical account of your death."

I had the opportunity to meet Borges in 1982, when he was giving a lecture at the New York Institute for the Humanities. He was a shy, fragile-seeming gentleman who said he couldn't imagine himself living in a bookless world. "I need books," he said. "They mean everything to me."

The chief event in his life, he once wrote, was his father's library, and in 1955, he was appointed director of Argentina's National Library. As he grew increasingly blind, he relied on family, friends, and assistants to read aloud to him every day.

Among the authors Borges said he loved most were Kafka, H. G. Wells, and G. K. Chesterton, suggesting that he felt more of an affinity with storytellers who shared his own "amazement at things" than with so-called avant-garde writers and theorists.

When he began writing himself, his prose was baroque. Now, he said in 1982, "I try to write in very simple words. When I was young, I used to think the invention of metaphor was possible. Now I don't except for very essential ones: stars and eyes, life and dreams, death and sleeping, time and the river."

Having made a promise to his mother years earlier, he added that he has continued to say the Lord's Prayer every night. "I don't know whether there's anybody at the other end of the line, but being an agnostic means all things are possible, even God. This world is so strange, anything may happen or may not happen. Being an agnostic makes me live in a larger, more futuristic kind of world. It makes me more tolerant."

The Moth Presents

ALL THESE WONDERS

True Stories About Facing the Unknown

(2017)

Edited by Catherine Burns

T he storytelling phenomenon *The Moth* was founded in 1997
by the writer George Dawes Green; its name comes from his
memories of growing up in St. Simons Island, Georgia, where
neighbors would gather late at night on a friend's porch to tell stories
and drink bourbon as moths flew in through the broken screens
and circled the porch light. *The Moth* went on to become a Peabody
Award–winning radio show and has since grown into what its artistic
director, Catherine Burns, calls "a modern storytelling movement"
that has inspired "tens of thousands of shows worldwide in places as
diverse as Tajikistan, Antarctica, and Birmingham, Alabama."

Participants have included well-known authors like Richard
Price, George Plimpton, Annie Proulx, and Christopher Hitchens
and scores of people from every background imaginable—scientists,
writers, teachers, soldiers, cowboys, comedians, and inventors,
among myriad others. The stories are "true, as remembered by the
storyteller," and are performed live.

The forty-five stories collected in *The Moth Presents All These
Wonders: True Stories About Facing the Unknown* translate
remarkably well to the page. They are stories that chronicle the
startling varieties and travails of human experience and the shared
threads of love, loss, fear, and kindness that connect us. Some are

urgent and raw. Some are elliptical and wry. Some are laugh-out-loud funny. And some are shattering in their sadness. But while the stories vary greatly in tone and voice, there is little sarcasm or snark. The emphasis is on communicating with the audience, with sharing an experience, a memory, a moment of grace.

Moth stories can be seen as part of the oral storytelling tradition dating back to Homer, but the personal nature of the tales—and their air of spontaneity—owes as much to stand-up comedy, blogging, talk-show anecdotes, and group therapy. They are not random reminiscences, however, but closely focused, finely tuned narratives that have the force of an epiphany, conveying with astonishing candor and fervor the familiar or the startling and the strange.

In "Unusual Normality," Ishmael Beah—who lost his family to war in Sierra Leone and became a child soldier at age thirteen—relates how he was adopted by an American woman when he was seventeen and how he attempted to fit in at school in New York. For instance, he did not tell his new classmates why he was so adept at paintball: "I wanted to explain certain things, but I felt that if they knew about my background, they would no longer allow me to be a child. They would see me as an adult, and I worried that they would fear me.

"My silence allowed me to experience things, to participate in my childhood, to do things I hadn't been able to do as a child."

Other stories pivot around a relationship between two people: the scientist Christof Koch and his longtime collaborator Francis Crick (who together with James Watson discovered the structure of DNA); Stephanie Peirolo and her son RJ, who suffered a traumatic brain injury after his car was struck at a blind intersection; the actor John Turturro and his troubled brother Ralph, who lives at the Creedmoor Psychiatric Center in Queens; Suzi Ronson, a hairdresser from a London suburb, who cut the young David Bowie's hair, joined his tour, and went on to become a music producer.

One of the most moving tales is "Fog of Disbelief" by Carl Pillitteri, who was working as a field engineer on the Fukushima Daiichi nuclear generating station in Japan when a devastating earthquake and tsunami hit the island in 2011, resulting in the worst nuclear disaster since Chernobyl; it left some 18,490 people dead or missing and led to the evacuation of more than 300,000.

After checking on his crew and colleagues, Pillitteri became concerned about the older woman who ran the restaurant where he ate five or six times a week. He spoke no Japanese, she spoke no English, and he and his friends knew her, fondly, only as the "Chicken Lady." The little building housing her restaurant was badly cracked by the quake, and she was nowhere to be found— even months later, when Pillitteri returned to the exclusion zone from America to look for her. Eventually, he enlisted the help of *The Japan Times* in tracking her down and learned that her name was Mrs. Owada.

Almost a year after the quake, he received a letter from her: "I have escaped from the disasters and have been doing fine every day. Pillitterisan, please take care of yourself. I know your work must be important. I hope you enjoy a happy life like you seemed to have when you came to my restaurant. Although I won't be seeing you, I will always pray for the best for you."

THE PLAGUE

(1947)

Albert Camus
Translated by Stuart Gilbert

E nduring classics speak not only to the circumstances of
the day in which they were written but across the decades
or centuries—uncannily anticipating our own experiences
and world today. Such is the case of Albert Camus's startlingly
resonant 1947 novel *The Plague (La Peste)*, a novel that can be read,
in Camus's own words, as both a tale about an epidemic and as an
allegory about the Nazi occupation of France and a "prefiguration
of any totalitarian regime, no matter where."

Camus was a dedicated member of the Resistance, who believed
there was a moral imperative to stand up to the Nazi occupation
of France. Inspired in part by his reading of *Moby-Dick,* he wanted
to investigate the metaphysical problem of evil, and his novel
chronicles how various characters react to the sudden arrival of
plague in Oran, crashing down on their heads as if "from a blue
sky." He described the arc of the pandemic—from denial to fear and
perseverance—with what many contemporary readers will recognize
as remarkable verisimilitude: government efforts to downplay the
threat giving way to mounting deaths and a quarantine; a shared
sense of isolation vying with a "sense of injustice" kindled by
profiteering and confusion; and for the poor, further deprivation. He
described worries about medical supplies, the daily hunt for food,
and the growing feelings of futility among "people marking time."

The duration and monotony of a quarantine, Camus wrote, has a way of turning people into "sleepwalkers" who dope "themselves with work" or who find the heightened emotions of the first weeks devolving into despondency and detachment, numbed by the arithmetic of death. For those who lived through a pestilence, he observed, the "grim days of plague" feel like "the slow, deliberate progress of some monstrous thing" crushing everything in its path.

Like members of the Resistance, Camus's narrator Dr. Rieux believes that "the habit of despair is worse than despair itself" and argues that the town's residents must not succumb to feelings of numbness and resignation. They must recognize the plague for what it is and dismiss the reflexive notion that such a catastrophe is "unthinkable" in a modern, supposedly advanced society like theirs.

Dr. Rieux knew "there must be no bowing down" to the plague— no compromise with evil, no resignation to fate. He identified with victims of the plague—"there was not one of their anxieties in which he did not share, no predicament of theirs that was not his." And he knew the "essential thing was to save the greatest possible number of persons from dying."

In the end, *The Plague* emerges as a testament to the dedication of individuals like Dr. Rieux and a group of volunteers who risk their lives to help victims of the plague. Dr. Rieux insists there is nothing heroic about his work—it is simply "a matter of common decency," which in his case consists of doing his job.

It's this sense of individual responsibility, combined with his feelings of solidarity with others, that enables Dr. Rieux to hold fast to two not entirely contradictory truths: the understanding that we must remain ever vigilant because "the plague bacillus," like the poison of fascism or tyranny, "never dies or disappears," and the optimistic belief that "what we learn in time of pestilence" is "that there are more things to admire in men than to despise."

THE PASSAGE OF POWER

The Years of Lyndon Johnson

(2012)

Robert A. Caro

R obert A. Caro has said that he was not really interested in
writing biographies; he was interested in writing "studies in
political power." This was true not only of his monumental
first book, *The Power Broker: Robert Moses and the Fall of New York,*
but also of the project that has consumed more than four decades of
his life: the voluminous and so far unfinished portrait of the thirty-
sixth president of the United States, Lyndon Baines Johnson.

As of 2019, Caro was still at work on the fifth—and presumably
final—volume of that biography dealing with LBJ's disastrous
handling of the war in Vietnam. In the meantime, volume 4, *The
Passage of Power,* stands as a model of the art of biography,
showcasing all of Caro's talents as a writer: his instinctive sense
of narrative, his ability to help readers feel history in the making,
and his gift for situating events within the context of their times.

The volume starts with Johnson's being catapulted into the White
House in the wake of the assassination of John F. Kennedy. It's an
extraordinarily dramatic—and pivotal—moment in American
history, and Caro conveys, on a visceral level, the magnitude of the
challenges LBJ faced on entering the White House.

Caro observes that Johnson first had to instill confidence in a
confused and grieving nation, and he needed to give the world—
in the midst of a cold war that had turned dangerously hot with

the Cuban missile crisis—a sense of continuity. To do so, he had to persuade key Kennedy administration members to stay on and to rally behind him. And he had to take on his many doubters, including liberals who questioned his commitment to civil rights and southerners who sought to block his social initiatives.

Johnson's knowledge of the tactical and strategic levers he could press; his personal relationships with Congressional power brokers; and his bare-knuckled willingness to bully, cajole, horse-trade, whatever it took to get what he wanted—these were the qualities, Caro observes, that enabled LBJ to overcome "congressional resistance and the power of the South" that had stood "in the path of social justice for a century."

Caro gives us an intimate understanding of how Johnson used the crisis of Kennedy's death and his own political acumen to push through Congress his predecessor's stalled tax-cut bill and civil rights legislation and to lay the groundwork for his own revolutionary War on Poverty. Caro also uses his accumulated knowledge of Johnson's personality—his insecurities, his fear of failure, his need to pander to superiors and dominate his inferiors—to examine the role that character plays in politics and policy making.

Johnson emerges as both a Shakespearean personage—with epic ambitions and epic flaws—and a more human-scale puzzle: needy, deceitful, brilliant, cruel, vulgar, idealistic, boastful, self-pitying, and blessed with such titanic energy that Abe Fortas once remarked, "The guy's just got extra glands." He was a man driven by a colossal ego and by a genuine sense of compassion for the powerless and the poor that had been forged by his own childhood. He was a man who, in the weeks and months after the assassination of JFK, was able to overcome his own weaknesses and baser instincts—in Caro's words, not for long but "long enough"—to act in a fashion that was "a triumph not only of genius but of will."

PURSUITS OF HAPPINESS
The Hollywood Comedy of Remarriage

(1981)

Stanley Cavell

This book will change how you watch Hollywood romantic comedies. It will make you see the Shakespearean underpinnings of such captivating screwball comedies as *The Philadelphia Story, His Girl Friday,* and *The Lady Eve* and more recent romantic comedies like *Crazy Rich Asians.* It will also leave you with a new understanding of some of the classic tropes found in comedy across the centuries—like its use of crisis (the same sort of event that serves as a catalyst for disaster in tragedy) as a spur to the resolution of confusion and misunderstanding.

Hollywood's brightest comedies from the 1930s and 1940s not only featured spirited heroines, reminiscent of Shakespeare's Beatrice and Rosalind, but also fast, witty exchanges between men and women that recall the animated banter in *Much Ado About Nothing.* The narrative movement in these films from conflict to confusion to eventual reconciliation parallels, in many ways, the structure of Shakespeare's romantic comedies, and in *Pursuits of Happiness,* the scholar Stanley Cavell used Northrop Frye's famous studies of the playwright's work to bolster his own arguments. Noting that Frye "calls particular attention to the special nature of the forgiving and forgetting" asked for at the end of traditional comedies, Cavell points out that *Bringing Up Baby* and *Adam's Rib* also conclude explicitly with requests for grace, and *The Awful Truth* and *The Philadelphia Story* do so symbolically.

Even the retreat to what Frye called "the green world" (a place where the rules of day-to-day life are suspended) that takes place in *A Midsummer Night's Dream* has its counterpart in these Hollywood comedies. As Cavell cleverly notes, *Bringing Up Baby, The Awful Truth, Adam's Rib,* and *The Lady Eve* all feature sequences in a distant place where perspective and renewal can be achieved—a setting, in these films, that usually turns out to be Connecticut.

Cavell, a philosopher who taught for decades at Harvard University, can be pretentious and heavy-handed: he analyzes Frank Capra in terms of Kant, compares Leo McCarey with Nietzsche, and brings up Locke's Second Treatise of Government in a discussion of *His Girl Friday*. But please persevere—even if that means skimming over some of the denser passages in this book. Cavell provides a hilarious explication of the copious double entendres in Howard Hawks's *Bringing Up Baby* and a provocative examination of the meaning of songs in *The Lady Eve, Adam's Rib,* and *The Awful Truth*. More important, he encourages us to appreciate the complexity of these great Hollywood films, and their delightful reinvention of comedic premises and techniques pioneered centuries ago by Shakespeare in *A Midsummer Night's Dream, The Winter's Tale,* and *All's Well That Ends Well*.

CAN'T WE TALK ABOUT SOMETHING MORE PLEASANT?

A Memoir

(2014)

Roz Chast

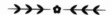

R oz Chast's people are worriers. They worry that they are too angry or too wimpy, too pushy or too passive or too passive-aggressive. They are afraid of driving, and afraid of chickens. They worry about Ebola turning up on West Eighty-Third Street in Manhattan.

Her cartoons—most of which have appeared in *The New Yorker* over the past several decades—capture the absurdities of contemporary life, the insecurities, neuroses, existential anxieties, and narcissistic complaints of the sorts of city dwellers made nervous by shopping malls and the great outdoors.

Though Chast writes as both a satirist and a social anthropologist, her work has long evinced an autobiographical impulse, drawing upon her experiences as a daughter, wife, and mother. And in her 2014 book, *Can't We Talk About Something More Pleasant?*, she tackled the subject of her parents—and her own efforts to help them navigate the jagged shoals of old age and ill health—with humor and raw candor. Her fondness for the exclamatory (expressed in capital letters, underlined words, and multiple exclamation points) is cranked up several notches here, and her familiar, scribbly people go from looking merely frazzled and put-upon to looking like the

Though Chast writes as both a satirist and a social anthropologist, her work has long evinced an autobiographical impulse, drawing upon her experiences as a daughter, wife, and mother.

shrieking figure in Munch's *Scream*—panicked and terrified as they see the abyss of loss and mortality looming just up the road.

Chast's descriptions of her parents are so sharply detailed that we instantly feel we've known them—as neighbors or family—for decades: her bossy, impossibly stubborn mother, Elizabeth, and her gentle, worrywart father, George, a couple who were in the same fifth-grade class and who, "aside from WWII, work, illness, and going to the bathroom," still did "everything together."

For decades, George and Elizabeth continued to live in Brooklyn ("Not the Brooklyn of artists or hipsters," but "the Brooklyn of people who have been left behind by everything and everyone") in the same apartment where the author grew up. The "to do" list of her childhood and adolescence, she recalls, included exhortations like "Avoid contact with other children" (because they might have germs), "Look up symptom in Merck Manual," and "Do not die."

After marrying and moving to Connecticut, Chast says she spent the 1990s avoiding Brooklyn. She began to realize, however, that her parents "were slowly leaving the sphere of TV commercial old age" ("SPRY! TOTALLY INDEPENDENT! JUST LIKE A NORMAL

ADULT, BUT WITH SILVER HAIR!!!") and moving into "the part of old age that was scarier" and harder to talk about.

Chast pulls no punches here. She chronicles her father's habit of chain-worrying, and her mother's bad temper and insistence on stocking up on useless bargains (like quintuple-queen-sized lobster bisque stockings because they're 80 percent off) while scrimping on necessities like a safe, reliable new space heater. She writes about moving her mother and father out of their home of forty-eight years, and about the decades of stuff left behind in their apartment— geologic layers of unopened mail, take-out menus, old books, old clothes, old *Life* magazines, empty Styrofoam egg cartons, antique appliances, and equally ancient Band-Aid boxes and jar lids. And she also chronicles her own flailing efforts to deal with the situation— her acute feelings of anxiety, worry, frustration, and sense of being completely overwhelmed.

Chast's drawings, photos, and text all come together to create a powerful collage memorial to her parents. Like Art Spiegelman's *Maus,* Marjane Satrapi's *Persepolis,* and Alison Bechdel's *Fun Home,* this book helps stretch the definition of the so-called graphic novel and underscores the possibilities of that genre as an innovative platform for autobiography and urgent, complex storytelling.

BOOKS BY BRUCE CHATWIN

IN PATAGONIA (1977)

WHAT AM I DOING HERE (1989)

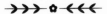

Writers of books, Bruce Chatwin observed in a posthumously published essay, fall into two categories: "the ones who 'dig in' and the ones who move." Among the members of the first category, he counted "Flaubert and Tolstoy labouring in their libraries; Zola with a suit of armour alongside his desk; Poe in his cottage; Proust in the cork-lined room." Among the movers, he named "Melville, who was 'undone' by his gentlemanly establishment in Massachusetts, or Hemingway, Gogol or Dostoyevsky whose lives, whether from choice or necessity, were a headlong round of hotels and rented rooms— and, in the case of the last, a Siberian prison."

Chatwin, of course, belongs firmly in the movers category.

He recalls he grew up with wanderlust in his DNA. His grandmother's cousin Charley, who became British consul in Punta Arenas, Chile, was shipwrecked at the entrance to the Strait of Magellan in 1898; his uncle Geoffrey was an Arabist and desert traveler who received a golden headdress from Emir Faisal, and his uncle Humphrey came to a "sad end in Africa."

With his father away in the navy, young Bruce spent his childhood drifting about England with his mother, staying with assorted relatives and friends. He later became a devoted "addict of atlases" and after leaving a promising job at Sotheby's, he decided to hit the road himself as a journalist.

His first book, *In Patagonia,* was a sensation. Its collage-like narrative, its lapidary prose, its mapping of a landscape that was as much a place in the writer's imagination as a set of coordinates on the globe—these qualities helped expand the boundaries of travel writing and revitalize the genre. The book's opening would be widely admired and cited: how a strange piece of leathery animal skin in his grandmother's cabinet—what he thought of as "a piece of brontosaurus" that had been found in Patagonia by his grandmother's cousin—lodged itself in young Bruce's mind, igniting a fascination with that distant land and a determination to one day journey there.

Chatwin's keen eye for the magical, the incongruous, and the exotic are also showcased in the profiles, essays, and travel pieces collected in *What Am I Doing Here.* Even the flimsier entries in this volume showcase Chatwin's gift of observation and his assurance in writing about anything—from Russian avant-garde art to survival tactics in the third world to rivalries in the world of high fashion. His best pieces read like small, perfectly shaped fictions peopled with startling characters. We meet the writer Nadezhda Mandelstam complaining about the lack of grand writers in Russia and asking Chatwin to please bring her some "real TRASH" to read, and Diana Vreeland sipping vodka and mistaking "Wales" for "whales."

André Malraux, sitting on the edge of his chair and wearing "a light brown jacket with lapels like butterfly wings," is described as a "talented young esthete who transformed himself into a great man." And Werner Herzog comes across as "a compendium of contradictions: immensely tough yet vulnerable, affectionate and remote, austere and sensual, not particularly well adjusted to the strains of everyday life but functioning efficiently under extreme conditions."

The less famous people in this volume are just as vividly portrayed: "a tall, almost skeletal, German mathematician and geographer" who has spent half of her seventy-two years in the Peruvian desert surveying the archaeological phenomenon known as the Nazca lines; a scrawny Tibetan smuggler doggedly embarking on a journey that will lead him across two glaciers and up a nineteen-thousand-foot pass; a botanist and explorer who likes to play Caruso records for mountain villagers in China.

Chatwin clearly felt an affinity with these solitary adventurers who left civilization behind for the outer limits of the world. Indeed his own life was animated by the fiercely held belief he shared with the Sherpas of Tibet, who are "compulsive travelers" and who mark their tracks with cairns and prayer flags, "reminding you that Man's real home is not a house, but the Road, and that life itself is a journey to be walked on foot."

 *His first book,* IN PATAGONIA, *was a sensation. Its collage-like narrative, its lapidary prose, its mapping of a landscape that was as much a place in the writer's imagination as a set of coordinates on the globe—these qualities helped expand the boundaries of travel writing and revitalize the genre.*

THE SLEEPWALKERS
How Europe Went to War in 1914

(2012)

Christopher Clark

W orld War I was a cataclysm that resulted in twenty million military and civilian deaths and the wounding of twenty-one million. It helped catalyze the Russian Revolution, set the stage for the rise of Nazism and World War II, and planted the seeds of many of today's intractable conflicts in the Middle East. And as Paul Fussell observed in his brilliant 1975 book, *The Great War and Modern Memory,* the brutalities of trench warfare would send shock waves throughout European culture, effectively shredding the old order and giving birth to modernism and its discontents.

"I shall never be able to understand how it happened," the writer Rebecca West later said of World War I. How did the assassination in Sarajevo of Archduke Franz Ferdinand, the presumptive heir to the throne of the Austro-Hungarian Empire, and his wife, Sophie, on June 28, 1914, push a peaceful Europe into war, and how did that war snowball into a conflagration that would consume the Continent and reconfigure the world?

Such questions are especially timely today, given the myriad ways in which the pre–World War I era resembles our own: it, too, was a time when globalization and new technologies like the telephone were creating seismic changes, and those changes, in turn, were fueling a growing populism. Right-wing, nationalistic movements were on the rise, and larger geopolitical shifts were threatening the stability of the world order.

"What must strike any twenty-first-century reader who follows the course of the summer crisis of 1914 is its raw modernity," the historian Christopher Clark writes in his compelling book *The Sleepwalkers*. An "extra-territorial" terrorist organization—built around "a cult of sacrifice, death and revenge"—was behind the assassination of Archduke Ferdinand, Clark writes, and the path to war was fueled by the dynamics of a complex landscape that featured "declining empires and rising powers"—a landscape not unlike the one we inhabit today.

Clark writes with thoughtful authority, judiciously sifting through the massive amount of information on the war, focusing on how (not why) decisions were reached and how various roads to peace or compromise were closed off. He does not try to assign blame for the war, and says there are no single smoking guns that can explain what happened. Instead, he argues that "the outbreak of war was the culmination of chains of decisions made by political actors" in different countries—decisions that were often based on misunderstandings, fragmentary or incomplete information, and the ideological and partisan positions of leading political actors.

Clark, who teaches at the University of Cambridge, uses his easy familiarity with European history to examine how each of the principal players in the rush to war—Germany, Austria-Hungary, France, Britain, Serbia—had long-standing preconceptions and suspicions about their rivals (and allies) that had been shaped by history and cultural traditions. He goes on to analyze how those reflexive attitudes could lead to bad decision making and how partisan domestic politics (like lobbying from nationalist pressure groups within each country) sometimes resulted in clashes among different factions of a country's foreign policy machinery.

Clark is also adept at drawing portraits of individual players in the buildup to war. Like the British foreign secretary Sir Edward Grey, who ensured that British policy "focused primarily on the 'German threat'" and who tried to shield "the policy-making process from the scrutiny of unfriendly eyes." And the erratic Wilhelm II, the German kaiser, who often "bypassed his responsible ministers by consulting with 'favorites,' encouraged factional strife" within his own government, and expounded views at odds with prevailing policy.

All these factors contributed to what Clark describes as the "ambient confusion" that swirled across the Continent in the days leading up to war—a war, in his words, that the European nations stumbled into, like sleepwalkers: "watchful but unseeing, haunted by dreams, yet blind to the reality of the horror they were about to bring into the world."

BOOKS ABOUT
FOREIGN POLICY AND
THE WORLD

THE RETREAT OF WESTERN LIBERALISM (2017)
Edward Luce

*A WORLD IN DISARRAY: American Foreign Policy
and the Crisis of the Old Order* (2017)
Richard Haass

*"Things fall apart; the centre cannot hold"—it's no surprise that these
ominous lines from William Butler Yeats's 1919 poem "The Second
Coming" were widely quoted a century after they were written.*

*With Brexit, the election of Donald Trump, and the surging tide of
nationalism and populism around the globe, the post–World War II
order—orchestrated by the United States and the Allies to help keep
the peace, and to promote democratic ideals and shared economic
prosperity—is threatened as never before. Authoritarianism is on
the rise, Trump has turned America from a stabilizing force into a
destabilizing one, Russia continues to interfere in the elections of
other nations in an effort to undermine liberal democracy, and an
authoritarian China is gaining power on the world stage.*

*What do these disquieting developments portend? What factors
will determine the resilience of democracy in the future? What lasting*

repercussions will domestic political upheavals—like those sustained by
the United States and Britain in 2016—have on global alignments? Two
highly informed books provide readers with a succinct understanding of
such developments on the world stage.

E dward Luce, the U.S. national editor and columnist at the
Financial Times, sees Trump and right-wing politicians in
Europe, like Marine Le Pen, not as causes of today's crisis
in democratic liberalism but as symptoms. Nor does he see Trump's
victory in 2016 as "an accident delivered by the dying gasp of America's
white majority—and abetted by Putin," after which regular political
programming will soon resume. Instead, Luce argues, Trump's election
is part of larger global trends, including the failure of two dozen
democracies since the turn of the millennium and growing downward
pressures on middle classes in the West (wrought by the accelerating
forces of globalization and automation and the fallout of the 2008
financial crisis) that are fueling nationalism and populist revolts.

The strongest glue holding liberal democracies together, Luce
argues, is economic growth, and when that growth stalls or fails,
things can take a dark, sudden turn. With growing competition
for jobs and resources, those he calls the "left-behinds" often seek
scapegoats for their woes, and consensus becomes harder to reach
as politics devolves into more and more of a zero-sum game.

"Many of the tools of modern life are increasingly priced beyond
most people's reach," Luce writes, pointing to the ballooning costs of
housing, health care, and a college degree. There is also rising income

inequality in the West; America, which "had traditionally shown the highest class mobility of any Western country, now has the lowest."

Trump's economic agenda (as opposed to his campaign rhetoric), Luce predicts, will "deepen the economic conditions that gave rise to his candidacy," while the "scorn he pours on democratic traditions at home" endangers the promotion of liberal democracy abroad. Luce also reminds us that Trump's embrace of autocrats (like Putin and Erdogan) and his dismissive treatment of NATO and longtime allies are leading to the squandering of whatever goodwill the United States still enjoyed abroad. Given this situation, Luce adds, "the stability of the planet—and the presumption of restraint—will have to rest in the hands of Xi Jinping and other powerful leaders," though he predicts that "chaos, not China, is likelier to take America's place."

Richard Haass, president of the Council on Foreign Relations, identifies a global trend of "declining order." "The twenty-first century will prove extremely difficult to manage," he writes in his lucid 2017 book, *A World in Disarray*, "representing as it does a departure from the almost four centuries of history—what is normally thought of as the modern era—that came before it."

After the end of the Cold War, Haass reminds us, a hopeful new world order did not emerge, as some giddily predicted in the wake of the fall of the Berlin Wall in 1989. Instead, the relative stability of a bipolar world—in which a nuclear-armed United States and Soviet Union approached each other with wary restraint—gave way to a complicated, multipolar one, subject to the forces of globalization, nuclear proliferation, and rapidly changing technology. In the new millennium, the growth of populism, extremist movements, and an assault on democratic institutions are contributing to further global instability.

Among the "worrisome developments" Haass describes are stepped-up rivalries among the world's major powers, the growing gap between global challenges (like climate change) and practical responses, and political dysfunction at home and abroad.

Writing with brisk authority, Haass moves fluently between discussions of larger dynamics and the specifics of tangled relationships in hot spots like Syria and Afghanistan. *A World in Disarray* provides an essential look at the current state of world affairs—put in perspective with a brief and compelling history of international relations from the Treaty of Westphalia (the pact signed in 1648, ending the Thirty Years' War) through the end of the Cold War and an equally concise analysis of the forces and events that have shaped today's global landscape.

In what may sound to readers like a warning to the Trump administration and its erratic approach to foreign and national security policy, Haass adds, "The United States has to be wary of sudden or sharp departures in what it does in the world. Consistency and reliability are essential attributes for a great power. Friends and allies who depend on the United States for their security need to know that this dependence is well placed. If America comes to be doubted, it will inevitably give rise to a very different and much less orderly world."

Disarray at home, he goes on, "is thus inextricably linked to disarray in the world." The two together, he concludes, "are nothing short of toxic."

BROTHER, I'M DYING

(2007)

Edwidge Danticat

America has always been a nation of immigrants, and many writers and thinkers who have played formative roles in American history and American letters were born abroad: from Thomas Paine and Alexander Hamilton, on through Vladimir Nabokov, Jacob Riis, Saul Bellow, and Isaac Asimov.

Even as Donald Trump has implemented cruel new immigration policies and used racist language to sow discord and division, polls continue to show that the majority of Americans (62 percent, according to a 2019 Pew survey) believe that immigrants strengthen the country with their talents and hard work. And the last several decades have witnessed an outpouring of stellar work about the immigrant experience by authors who are themselves immigrants or second-generation Americans, including Gary Shteyngart, Junot Díaz, Jhumpa Lahiri, Marlon James, Dinaw Mengestu, Ocean Vuong, Viet Thanh Nguyen, Téa Obreht, Colum McCann, and Yaa Gyasi. The work of such writers reminds us of the innovation, complexity, and dynamism that immigrants have brought to American culture. Often writing as outsiders, they are especially attuned to the promises and incongruities of the American dream, just as they tend to be keen observers, noticing aspects of everyday life that many of us shrug off or take for granted.

The work of Edwidge Danticat embodies this stereoscopic vision of America, while at the same time leaving us with an eloquent picture of the country of her birth and the painful legacy of Haiti's violent history.

When Danticat was two years old, she recalled in her 2007 memoir, *Brother, I'm Dying*, her father left Haiti for New York City. Two years later, her mother followed him to America, leaving Edwidge with ten new dresses she'd sewn, most of them too big for the little girl and meant to be worn in the years to come. During the following eight years Edwidge and her brother lived with her father's brother, Joseph, and his wife, Denise, in a Port-au-Prince neighborhood caught in the cross fire between rival gangs and political factions.

For years, Uncle Joseph, who'd become a devout Baptist, refused to leave Bel Air. It was only after local gangs burned and looted his church that the eighty-one-year-old Joseph smuggled himself out of the neighborhood and out of the country. His flight to America, however, soon turned into a nightmare. After reaching Miami and asking for asylum, he was sent to a Florida detention facility, where he fell ill and was transported to a hospital. He died a day later.

Although Joseph had never wanted to leave his beloved Haiti, he was buried in a cemetery in Queens, "exiled finally in death," becoming "part of the soil of a country that had not wanted him." It wasn't long before he was joined there by his brother, Mira, who had been suffering from end-stage pulmonary fibrosis. Two brothers who made very different choices in their lives and who ended up, side by side, in a graveyard in one of New York's outer boroughs.

In telling the stories of her father and her uncle, Danticat gives us an intimate sense of the personal consequences of the Haitian diaspora: its impact on parents and children, brothers and sisters, those who stay and those who leave.

Brother, I'm Dying is a haunting book about exile and family love, and how that love can survive distance and separation, loss and abandonment, and somehow endure, fierce and inviolate and shining.

UNDERWORLD

(1997)

Don DeLillo

No American novelist has been more attuned to the surreal weirdness of our recent history than Don DeLillo. In novels like *Players, Libra, Mao II, White Noise,* and his masterpiece *Underworld,* he used his razzle-dazzle gifts as a writer to create a vivid fever chart of American history, describing, with uncanny prescience, how random violence and paranoia had insinuated themselves into the collective unconscious, and how celebrities and terrorists were seizing hold of the national imagination.

DeLillo drew a portrait of America as a place where conspiracy thinking had replaced religion as an organizing principle, a place where the clammy "hand of coincidence" reached into everybody's life, a place where "the rules of what is thinkable" changed overnight. He described the seduction of technology and its ability to magnify the absurdities of pop culture, and the power of bomb makers and gunmen to seize headlines in a society distracted and benumbed by a surfeit of data and news and reeling from attention deficit disorder.

His novels anticipated the shock and horror of 9/11 and its dark, unspooling aftermath, as well as the growing power of crowds, which had begun to surge across the internet and would give rise to a growing mistrust of experts and elites.

DeLillo's dazzling symphonic novel *Underworld* brought together all his preoccupations in a phosphorescent narrative that captured the second half of the twentieth century in an America living under the shadow of the atomic bomb and looking ahead to the upheavals of the new millenium.

Though *Underworld* pivots around the experiences of one Nick Shay, a hero who shares his creator's Bronx childhood and Roman Catholic upbringing, it unfolds into a panoramic portrait of America, charting the intersecting lives of dozens of characters, famous and obscure—sports fans and conspiracy fanatics, hustlers, con men, businessmen, scientists, and artists—while leaving us with a visceral sense of how the personal and the collective can converge with explosive force. The novel's opening sequence alone stands as one of the great tours de force in modern fiction, capturing the shared experience of more than thirty-four thousand baseball fans watching the classic October 3, 1951, ball game in which the Giants beat the Dodgers to win the pennant race—a scene that DeLillo uses as a jumping-off point for tracing the long arc of history in the remainder of that century.

Underworld is a novel that showcases DeLillo's copious talents: his gift for eerie, dead-on dialogue that's part Richard Price, part David Mamet, and part overheard-on-the-subway; his radar for the radioactive image that will sear itself into a reader's mind; his jazzy, synesthesic prose; and his cinematic ability to convey the simultaneity of experience, how the past and the present, the momentous and the trivial, run on an endless loop in our minds. Borrowing techniques of collage and improvisation and montage from painting, music, and film, the novel's fragmented narrative reflects the very discordances and discontinuities that define so much of contemporary life.

In an earlier book, a DeLillo character talked about a Joycean novel "in which nothing is left out," a novel that might capture the nervous spin and drift of recent American history and freeze forever in words a past that never stops happening. With *Underworld*, DeLillo achieved exactly that.

THE BRIEF WONDROUS
LIFE OF OSCAR WAO

(2007)

Junot Díaz

T he first thing that hits you about Junot Díaz's 2007 novel, *The Brief Wondrous Life of Oscar Wao,* is his electric voice: language that's part caffeinated street slang and part hyperventilated Spanglish; magic, kinetic prose that leaps off the page and that's elastic enough to enable Díaz to talk about anything from Tolkien to Trujillo, anime movies to the horrors of Caribbean history, sexual escapades at Rutgers University to violent police raids in Santo Domingo. It's language that underscores how Díaz's characters commute between two worlds: the Dominican Republic, the ghost-haunted motherland that shapes their nightmares and their dreams; and America (a.k.a. New Jersey), the land of freedom and hope (and sometimes disappointment) they've fled to as part of the great Dominican diaspora.

By turns funny and heartbreaking, touching and street-smart, this remarkable debut novel evolves from a comic portrait of a second-generation Dominican geek into a haunting meditation on public and private history and the weight of the past. It looks at how immigration to America affects several generations of a family: parents, fleeing violence and oppression at home, and struggling to invent new lives for themselves in the land of malls and suburbs, where everything feels foreign; and their children, immersed in

American pop culture and their youthful frustrations in romance and school, even as they recognize the absurd gap between their daily concerns and the devastating choices their parents and grandparents faced back home. For these characters, the past is both an anchor, tying them to cherished family roots, and a dangerous undertow, threatening to pull them under with traumatic and crippling memories.

For these characters, the past is both an anchor, tying them to cherished family roots, and a dangerous undertow, threatening to pull them under with traumatic and crippling memories.

Oscar, Díaz's homely homeboy hero, is "not one of those Dominican cats everybody's always going on about—he wasn't no home-run hitter or a fly bachatero, not a playboy" with a million hot girls on the line. Oscar is an overweight, self-loathing nerd and science-fiction fanatic who dreams of becoming "the Dominican Tolkien." He pines after girls who ignore him and worries he will die a virgin, despite the efforts of his beautiful sister Lola, a "Banshees-loving punk chick," and his macho college roommate Yunior to get him to diet, exercise, and "stop talking crazy negative." Yunior wonders if Oscar, like his mother, is living under a House of Atreus–like curse—a "high-level fukú" placed on the family by the Dominican dictator Rafael Trujillo.

As the novel progresses, we—like Oscar—are drawn further and further into his family's past. We learn that his mother Beli's hard-nosed street cred is rooted in a Dominican childhood of almost unimaginable pain and loss: her wealthy father was tortured and incarcerated by Trujillo's thugs; her mother, run over by a truck after her husband's imprisonment. Beli, herself, would barely escape from the island with her life, after having an ill-fated affair with a dangerous man who was married to Trujillo's sister.

Here is Díaz writing about Trujillo: "Homeboy dominated Santo Domingo like it was his very own private Mordor; not only did he lock the country away from the rest of the world, isolate it behind the Plátano Curtain, he acted like it was his very own plantation, acted like he owned everything and everyone, killed whomever he wanted to kill. . . . His Eye was everywhere; he had a Secret Police that out-Stasi'd the Stasi, that kept watch on everyone, even those everyones who lived in *the States*."

Díaz's galvanic novel illuminates the sorrows of Dominican history while at the same time intimately chronicling the dreams and losses of one family. It's a book that transcends all conventional literary genres and brackets, fusing magical realism with postmodern pyrotechnics, sci-fi memes with historical facts, a novel that decisively established Díaz as one of contemporary fiction's most powerful and enthralling voices.

BOOKS BY JOAN DIDION

SLOUCHING TOWARDS BETHLEHEM (1968)

THE WHITE ALBUM (1979)

J oan Didion's 1968 collection of essays, *Slouching Towards Bethlehem,* took its title from Yeats's famous poem "The Second Coming"—the one with the lines "Things fall apart; the centre cannot hold; / Mere anarchy is loosed upon the world." She wrote that the lines reverberated in her "inner ear as if they were surgically implanted there"; they spoke to her sense that the world as she "had understood it no longer existed," that things had stopped making sense, that chaos and randomness—what she called "dice theory"— were ascendant.

Didion's essays in *Slouching Towards Bethlehem* and its 1979 bookend, *The White Album* (which took its title from the Beatles' album), gave us indelible snapshots of the craziness that was abroad in America in the 1960s and 1970s—from the migration of flower children to San Francisco's Haight-Ashbury, to the terror of the Manson murders, to the dread and emotional vertigo Didion was herself feeling in those unsettling days.

"You are getting a woman who somewhere along the line misplaced whatever slight faith she ever had in the social contract, in the meliorative principle," she wrote in *The White Album*. She felt she had become "a sleepwalker," alert only "to the stuff of bad dreams, the children burning in the locked car in the supermarket parking lot," the freeway sniper, the hustlers, the insane, "the lost children, all the ignorant armies jostling in the night."

Decades later, her worst fears about "the unspeakable peril of the everyday" were realized when John Gregory Dunne, her husband of nearly forty years, suddenly died of a massive heart attack and their only child, Quintana, died less than two years later, after months in and out of hospitals—heartbreaking losses that Didion would chronicle in *The Year of Magical Thinking* and *Blue Nights*.

I first read Joan Didion in Tom Wolfe's groundbreaking 1973 anthology, *The New Journalism*—one of those books, along with *Smiling Through the Apocalypse: Esquire's History of the Sixties*, that made many of us want to become journalists. When I hunted down a copy of *Slouching Towards Bethlehem*, I was blown away by Didion's voice and the idiosyncratic power of her prose—its surgical precision, its almost incantatory rhythms. Her fascination with "extreme and doomed commitments" and her awareness of "the edge" also resonated with my teenager's melodramatic imagination.

F. Scott Fitzgerald had pioneered the personal essay with "The Crack-Up" decades earlier, but Didion's candor felt somehow new; in fact her work anticipated, in many ways, the memoir writing that would be embraced by a new generation of writers in the 1990s and the first decades of the twenty-first century.

In one of her signature essays, Didion wrote about the importance of remembering "what it was to be me," and whether she was writing about love or marriage or starting out as a journalist in New York, she spoke to the experiences of many young women in the 1970s and 1980s. She wrote about what it was like to be a reporter who happened to be shy and small and "temperamentally unobtrusive." She described her nearly empty New York apartment and hanging "fifty yards of yellow theatrical silk across the bedroom windows, because I had some idea that the gold light would make me feel better." She knew how to travel alone in dangerous countries like El Salvador and Colombia, and she also knew the sorts of things my mother would have liked me to know: how to make bouillabaisse and borscht, or recall the provenance of a given dress, be it from Peck & Peck or Bonwit Teller, or I. Magnin in L.A.

I was lucky enough to interview Didion in 1979 about *The White Album*. It was a freelance piece and the first thing I ever wrote for *The New York Times*. When I arrived at her home in Brentwood, California, I eagerly took out my reporter's notebook and scribbled down all the "Didion-esque" details: the yellow Corvette, just like the one Maria drives in *Play It as It Lays*, parked in the driveway; and the avocado tree in the backyard that Didion's exterminator had told her was a magnet for rats.

In *The White Album* and *Slouching Towards Bethlehem*, Didion used her own anxieties and experiences as a kind of index to the American zeitgeist. She wrote about how the California she knew growing up in Sacramento had metamorphosed overnight into a new California—the old frontier ways giving way to Hollywood dinner parties and New Age retreats: the American faith in the possibility of reinventing oneself devolving into rootlessness and anomie. Writing was a way for Didion to try to impose a narrative on the disorder she saw around her, and a means of trying to understand the changes overtaking the country as it lurched through the traumas of Vietnam and Watergate and the assassinations of Martin Luther King, Jr., and Robert F. Kennedy, as violence erupted on college campuses and in the streets of Chicago and Los Angeles, and it seemed, to her, that "everything was unmentionable but nothing was unimaginable."

Didion told me she had long wanted a house like her Brentwood two-story Colonial: "I wanted a house with a center-hall plan with the living room on your right and the dining hall on your left when you come in. I imagined if I had this house, a piece of order and peace would fall into my life, but order and peace did not fall into my life. Living in a two-story house doesn't take away the risks."

A HEARTBREAKING WORK OF
STAGGERING GENIUS

(2000)

Dave Eggers

D
ave Eggers's remarkable 2000 book, *A Heartbreaking Work of Staggering Genius,* is both staggering *and* heartbreaking. In recounting the story of how his father and his mother died within weeks of each other, and how, at the age of twenty-one, he became a surrogate parent to his eight-year-old brother Toph, Eggers wrote a head-swiveling "memoir-y kind of thing" that attested to his astonishing range as a writer—capable of shifting gears, effortlessly, in fact exuberantly, between the self-referential and the sincere, the hyperbolic and the earnest; and adept at writing in different keys that run the gamut between the comic and the meditative, the playful and the tender.

A Heartbreaking Work of Staggering Genius bears as much resemblance to conventional autobiographies as Laurence Sterne's digression-filled *Tristram Shandy* does to the conventional novel. Intent on trying to convey to the reader exactly what it felt like to lose both his parents and to become, at the same time, a parent to his little brother, Eggers embraced an arsenal of techniques, annotating and footnoting his stream-of-consciousness reminiscences and turning the sort of postmodernist narrative strategies most often found in cerebral, experimental works into unlikely but effective tools for communicating his grief and confusion—his contradictory emotions in wanting to record everything that happened while sometimes using hyperbole and satire, defensively, to avoid being overcome by loss.

"Our house sits on a sinkhole," he writes. "Our house is the one being swept up in the tornado, the little train-set model house floating helplessly, pathetically around in the howling black funnel. We're weak and tiny. We're Grenada. There are men parachuting from the sky."

After the death of their parents, Dave and Toph move out to Berkeley, California, to be near their elder sister, Beth. The brothers set up housekeeping as father and son and live in dorm-room-like squalor: books, papers, half-filled glasses of milk, old French fries, half-opened packages of pretzels and heaps of sports equipment (at least four basketballs, eight lacrosse balls, and a skateboard) strewn across the living room. An ant infestation in the kitchen. Laundry piled up, bills "paid in ninety days minimum," school forms submitted late.

On the odd occasion when Eggers leaves the house for a date, he worries that something terrible (basically whatever his "wild, horror-infested imagination" can concoct) will happen, that the babysitter will murder his brother or someone else will kill Toph and the babysitter. He lives now, he thinks, "in the zone of all probability": "I cannot be surprised. Earthquakes, locusts, poison rain would not impress me. Visits from God, unicorns, bat-people with torches and scepters—it's all plausible."

Eggers attends Toph's Little League games with the other kids' parents. He decides they need to cook dinner for themselves about four times a week (based on their mother's recipes), and he tries to teach Toph everything he loves.

"His brain is my laboratory, my depository," Eggers writes. "Into it I can stuff the books I choose, the television shows, the movies, my opinion about elected officials, historical events, neighbors, passersby. He is my twenty-four-hour classroom, my captive audience, forced to ingest everything I deem worthwhile." He reads Toph *Hiroshima* (leaving out the grisly parts), *Maus,* and *Catch-22,* teaches him tricks with the Frisbee, and instructs him in the fine art of sock sliding down their apartment's hallway.

Eggers has an uncommon ability to convey intense emotion— be it joy or anxiety or bereavement. He can turn a Frisbee game with his brother into an existential meditation on life. He can convey the wild, caffeinated joy he feels after seeing a friend wake up from a coma. And he can turn his efforts to scatter his mother's ashes in Lake Michigan into a story that's both a lyrical tribute to her passing and a manic, slapstick account of his ineptitude as a mourner, lugging about a canister of ashes that reminds him, creepily, of the Ark of the Covenant in the Spielberg movie.

This is a deeply affecting memoir about family love and resilience: a book that marked the debut of a prodigiously talented and inventive young writer. Promise that would be fulfilled with such compelling later works as *What Is the What* and *A Hologram for the King*—books whose very difference in tone and style would underscore the wide, variegated spectrum of Eggers's gifts.

THE COLLECTED STORIES OF DEBORAH EISENBERG

(2010)

D eborah Eisenberg's haunting short story "Twilight of the
Superheroes" takes place in a millennial New York City,
in the days and months before and after 9/11, mapping
how the city has changed and not changed, how things return to a
facsimile of normality, even though a hole remains in the skyline,
even though people remember how "the planes struck, tearing
through the curtain of that blue September morning, exposing the
dark world that lay right behind it."

"You see," a character named Nathaniel says, "if history has
anything to teach us, it's that—despite all our efforts, despite our
best (or worst) intentions, despite our touchingly indestructible
faith in our own foresight—we poor humans cannot actually think
ahead; there are just too many variables. And so, when it comes
down to it, it always turns out that no one is in charge of the things
that really matter."

A similar realization strikes many of Eisenberg's characters.
An accident, an illness, the abrupt ending of a relationship, or the
sudden crashing of expectations against reality—such unforeseen
developments leave these people with a heightened awareness of
the precariousness of life, the understanding that something good,
bad, or merely surprising can occur at any moment. In some cases,
it's a familial loss or revelation; in others, a larger public event with
personal reverberations.

In a later collection, "Your Duck Is My Duck," Eisenberg writes that the news of late often resembles "a magic substance in a fairy tale," producing "perpetually increasing awfulness from rock-bottom bad"—awfulness that seeps into the collective consciousness, at least among those with some sense of their own complicity in the world's unfairnesses and betrayals.

Using her playwright's ear for dialogue and unerring radar for the revealing detail, Eisenberg writes short stories that have the emotional amplitude of novels, giving us—in just a handful of pages—a visceral sense of her characters' everyday routines, the worlds they transit, and the families they rebel against or allow to define them. By moving fluently back and forth between the present and the past, she shows how memories and long-ago events shadow current decisions, how time—the relentless ticktock of daily life—both confines and liberates us.

Whether they are adolescents trying to navigate the passage to adulthood, young would-be artists roaming the globe, or older folks who see mortality looming on the horizon like an iceberg, they are people who experience themselves as outsiders, who feel poorly equipped, by temperament or past experience, for the roles they suddenly find themselves playing. They are given to trippy, stream-of-consciousness musings (on how tea bags work: "Did bits of water escort bits of tea from the bag, or what?") and melancholy philosophical asides ("Humans were born, they lived. They glued themselves together in little clumps, and then they died").

Instead of forcing her characters' stories into neat, arbitrary, preordained shapes, Eisenberg allows them to grow organically into oddly shaped, asymmetrical narratives that possess all the dismaying twists and surprising turns of real life.

THE WASTE LAND

(1922)

T. S. Eliot

Nearly a century after it was published, T. S. Eliot's *Waste Land* stands as one of the central pillars of modernism. Along with Joyce's *Ulysses* (also published in 1922), Stravinsky's *Rite of Spring,* Picasso's *Les Demoiselles d'Avignon,* and Virginia Woolf's stream-of-consciousness novels, the poem embodied Ezra Pound's exhortation to artists to "make it new!" The jagged, jump-cut energy of these works, their collage-like use of fragments, their embrace of dissonance and discontinuity, and their defiance of tradition and linearity—these elements mirrored the sense of alienation and turmoil the world was experiencing in the early years of the twentieth century as it grappled with convulsive social and political changes and the shattering fallout of World War I.

After decades of being taught in high school and college, after its innovations have been widely assimilated, imitated, and satirized, *The Waste Land* might now strike some readers as familiar, even trite. It's hard to appreciate just how radical it was when it was first published, breaking old rules of prosody and using new language and techniques to tackle what were then unfashionable themes of spiritual alienation and urban malaise.

But reread today, the poem's evocation of the broken world left in the wake of World War I remains remarkably resonant. It depicts a world in which the old rules and certainties have vanished— a spiritual desert where "the dead tree gives no shelter," where

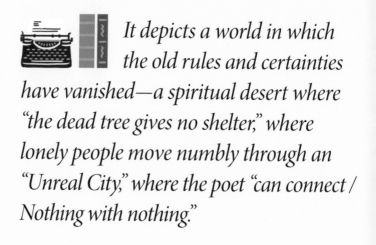 *It depicts a world in which the old rules and certainties have vanished—a spiritual desert where "the dead tree gives no shelter," where lonely people move numbly through an "Unreal City," where the poet "can connect / Nothing with nothing."*

lonely people move numbly through an "Unreal City," where the poet "can connect / Nothing with nothing."

Eliot once observed that the poem was written as "the relief of a personal . . . grouse against life," and it was, in part, a reflection of his own state of mind as he struggled with a miserable marriage and a nervous breakdown. But much the way that Kafka's work, which was rooted in his relationship with a domineering father, yielded lasting metaphors for modern life and politics, so did Eliot's *Waste Land* mirror larger dynamics in the world. It's a world not unlike our own, haunted by a sense of loss and dislocation— a world, to use words written by Eliot in an essay about *Ulysses,* that presented an "immense panorama of futility and anarchy" while thirsting for redemption and renewal.

BOOKS BY JOSEPH J. ELLIS

FOUNDING BROTHERS: The Revolutionary Generation (2000)

*AMERICAN CREATION: Triumphs and Tragedies at the
Founding of the Republic* (2007)

*REVOLUTIONARY SUMMER: The Birth of American
Independence* (2013)

AMERICAN DIALOGUE: The Founders and Us (2018)

No history book possesses the four-dimensional magic of Lin-Manuel Miranda's brilliant musical *Hamilton,* but for readers interested in learning more about the Revolutionary War era, these works by the historian Joseph J. Ellis are a good place to start.

In multiple books, Ellis has brought the founding era to life, giving us brisk accounts of pivotal events during the Revolutionary War and the walk-up to the Constitutional Convention, as well as succinct analyses of the ideas, ideals, and prejudices at work in those formative years. These are crucial subjects to understand today, given Donald Trump's assault on the very checks and balances put in place by the founders to protect our democracy, and given the tragic consequences of the founders' own failures to grapple with the nation's original sin of slavery.

The founding era, Ellis writes in his 2018 book *American Dialogue,* produced "the Big Bang that created all the planets and orbits in our political universe, thereby establishing the institutional framework for what is still an ongoing argument about our destiny as a people and a nation."

Ellis reminds us just how improbable the odds were of the American Revolution succeeding. The British army and navy constituted the most powerful military force in the world, while the Continental army, under Washington's command, was a ragtag band of men, often poorly equipped and trained, sometimes lacking shoes and suffering from malnutrition.

Circumstance and luck played a big role in shaping the decisions of American leaders, who were frequently making things up as they went along, teetering on the edge of the abyss.

Had fog not descended over New York City during the Battle of Brooklyn, would Washington have been able to achieve the remarkable feat of evacuating nearly ten thousand men from Brooklyn to Manhattan—across the East River, a body of water controlled by the daunting British navy?

Had Washington had more troops might he have taken a more confrontational approach toward the British army, instead of adopting the largely defensive posture he did after Valley Forge—a tactic, it turned out, that forced the British to fight for the sympathies of ordinary citizens in the sprawling countryside, drained British resources, and eventually helped turn the tide?

In recounting such developments, Ellis conveys how participants experienced the headlong rush of events as they happened, even as he pulls back, from time to time, to assess how their decisions made on the run would look in the rearview mirror of history.

He also underscores the crucial roles that character and individual decision making played both in ensuring that thirteen colonies became "We the People of the United States," and in bequeathing grievous social and political inequities that persist to this day.

In some cases, Ellis argues, the right people with the right skills happened to be there at the right moment in time: from Washington's stoic military leadership to James Madison's savvy as a political tactician to Alexander Hamilton's fiscal wisdom. With the Louisiana Purchase, however, Thomas Jefferson's racism and willful hypocrisy led him to pass up what Ellis calls "the most fortuitous opportunity history ever offered to implement a gradual emancipation policy that would put slavery on the road to extinction" and change "the direction of American history in accord with his own words in the Declaration of Independence."

As Ellis sees it, the ideological and temperamental differences of the founders—and their vociferous friendships and rivalries—created an intellectual ferment that enhanced creativity and "replicated the checks and balances of the Constitution with a human version of the same principle." They differed over the competing claims of federal and state sovereignty, and over the meaning of the American Revolution: whether it was about individual liberty and a clean break from British and European political traditions; or whether it meant "the virtuous surrender of personal, state and sectional interests to the larger purposes of American nationhood."

While Washington, Hamilton, Adams, Jefferson, Madison, and Franklin belonged to what Ellis describes as "the greatest generation of political talent in American history," they remain men of their day, limited by the mores of their times and their own biases and shortcomings. Looking back at their lives and decisions, Ellis writes, reminds us that the study of history is an interactive process—"an ongoing conversation between past and present."

THE FOUNDERS ON
AMERICAN DEMOCRACY

THE FEDERALIST PAPERS (1788)
Alexander Hamilton, James Madison, and John Jay

GEORGE WASHINGTON'S FAREWELL ADDRESS (1796)

*T*he *Federalist Papers* belong in the list of essential American documents, right near the top, after the Constitution, the Declaration of Independence, and the Bill of Rights, and they are necessary reading today, when the very institutions the founders established as the cornerstones of our democracy are increasingly coming under threat.

Orchestrated by the indefatigable Alexander Hamilton (who at the time was only thirty-some years old), the eighty-five essays were written in 1787 and 1788 by Hamilton, James Madison, and John Jay in an effort to help win ratification of the new Constitution. The essays (many of which first appeared in newspapers) are both an eloquent defense of the Constitution and a thoughtful amplification of the founders' thinking about how democracy in America would work.

The papers are informed by the founders' realistic assessment of human nature, their knowledge of the pitfalls that other democracies in history had stumbled into, and an awareness of the dangers America would likely face in the years to come. Hamilton warned that "dangerous ambition more often lurks behind the specious mask of zeal for the rights of the people," adding that of the despots in the past "who have overturned the liberties of republics, the greatest number have begun their career by paying obsequious court to the people; commencing demagogues, and ending tyrants." He also warned that partisan groups would try to win converts through "the loudness of their declamations and the bitterness of their invectives."

America was built on the Enlightenment ideals of reason, liberty, and progress, and the founders tried to fashion a government that would help contain the electorate's more extreme impulses and allow for the building of consensus over long-term goals (as opposed to short-term gratifications).

To Madison, one of the greatest dangers was the power of what he called "factions"—groups of citizens, united "by some common impulse of passion, or of interest," which are "adversed to the rights of other citizens, or to the permanent and aggregate interests of the community."

In Federalist No. 51, Madison wrote, "If men were angels, no government would be necessary. If angels were to govern men, neither external nor internal controls on government would be necessary. In framing a government which is to be administered by men over men, the great difficulty lies in this: you must first enable the government to control the governed, and in the next place oblige it to control itself."

Toward that end, the three branches of government—the executive, the legislative, the judicial—were designed by the founders to serve as checks and balances on one another. None of the branches, Madison wrote, "ought to possess, directly or indirectly, an overruling influence over the others."

For instance, the president was given the power to nominate ambassadors and judges of the Supreme Court, but only with the advice and consent of the Senate; in the case of making treaties with other countries, two-thirds of the Senate would have to sign on. Also, the president could be impeached and tried by the legislative branch and removed from office upon "conviction of treason, bribery, or other high crimes and misdemeanors." For these reasons, Hamilton argued, "there is a total dissimilitude" between the president of the United States and the king of Great Britain.

Most casual readers won't want to read all the essays in this volume, but the following are a good place to start: Hamilton's introduction (No. 1); Madison's essay on the dangers of factional politics (No. 10) and his chapter on checks and balances in the government (No. 51).

Also timely and relevant are Madison's detailed essays on the distribution of power among the three branches of government (Nos. 47–49) and Hamilton's chapters about checks on presidential power (No. 69) and the importance of an independent judiciary (No. 78).

Delivered some eight years later, in 1796, near the end of his second term as president, George Washington's Farewell Address (readily available online) is another indispensable document from the earliest days of the Republic, echoing many of the themes articulated in *The Federalist Papers*.

Washington's address was eerily clairvoyant about the perils the young nation might one day confront. In order to protect its future, he cautioned, the country must guard its Constitution and remain vigilant about efforts to sabotage the separation and balance of powers within the government that he and the other founders had so carefully crafted.

Washington warned about the rise of "cunning, ambitious, and unprincipled men" who might try "to subvert the power of the people" and "usurp for themselves the reins of government, destroying afterwards the very engines which have lifted them to unjust dominion."

He warned about "the insidious wiles of foreign influence" and the dangers of "ambitious, corrupted, or deluded citizens" who might devote themselves to a favorite foreign nation and "betray or sacrifice the interests" of America.

And, finally, Washington warned of the "continual mischiefs of the spirit of party," which are given to creating strife through "ill-founded jealousies and false alarms," and the perils that factionalism (East versus West, North versus South, state versus federal) posed to the unity of the country. Citizens, he said, must indignantly frown "upon the first dawning of every attempt to alienate any portion of our country from the rest, or to enfeeble the sacred ties which now link together the various parts."

INVISIBLE MAN

(1952)

Ralph Ellison

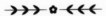

I am an invisible man." So begins Ralph Ellison's extraordinary
1952 novel. "No, I am not a spook like those who haunted Edgar
Allan Poe; nor am I one of your Hollywood-movie ectoplasms,"
his narrator goes on. "I am a man of substance, of flesh and bone, fiber
and liquids." He is invisible, he explains, "because people refuse to see
me. Like the bodiless heads you see sometimes in circus sideshows,
it is as though I have been surrounded by mirrors of hard, distorting
glass." When people look at him, they see "only my surroundings,
themselves, or figments of their imagination—indeed, everything and
anything except me."

Being invisible is a metaphor for being black in America: for being
ignored, persecuted, demeaned, subjected to different standards of
justice, and labeled with crude racial stereotypes. At the same time,
Ellison suggests, being invisible is an existential condition we all face
in trying to throw off the expectations and assumptions of other
people and define ourselves as individuals.

By turns realistic, fable-like, and hauntingly surreal, *Invisible
Man* is, at once, a visionary meditation on race and the
multicultural heritage of the United States and a vibrant modernist
bildungsroman—a Kafkaesque account of the narrator's journey
from naïveté to knowledge, from passivity to action, from credulity
to understanding.

That journey is a nightmarish one: the last twenty-odd years of the narrator's life have been a succession of betrayals. As a small-town high school student who has been instructed in the virtues of humility, he is subjected to a humiliating experience by the big-shot white people in town, who order him and a group of other black teenagers to fight one another, blindfolded, in a boxing ring. Though the narrator is given a scholarship to the state's black college, what he encounters there is also dispiriting: the university's president, Dr. Bledsoe, it turns out, holds on to power by pandering to white donors, declaring he would "have every Negro in the country hanging on tree limbs by morning if it means staying where I am."

Kicked out of college by Bledsoe, the narrator moves to New York City, where his misfortunes continue: his job at a factory—which manufactures "Optic White," the "best white paint in the world"—ends with his being sent to the factory hospital, where he is subjected to electric shock therapy that is supposed to erase his memory. Later, when he joins an organization called the Brotherhood (a left-wing group that sounds vaguely like the Communist Party), he is disillusioned to learn that its leaders, too, seem intent on using him for their own ends.

Ellison noted in an introduction that his hero shares certain traits with the narrator of Dostoyevsky's *Notes from Underground*, and the narrator comes to inhabit a cellar room lit with 1,369 lightbulbs. He is living in a "state of hibernation," trying to make sense of his life and preparing "for action." He has decided that he has "a socially responsible role to play" and that he will tell his story—the one set forth in these pages—and describe what he has learned in the course of his peregrinations.

What he has learned is that he is "nobody but myself"; no longer will he allow himself to be defined by others, black or white.

And far from being embittered by his experiences, he says he has realized that "too much of your life will be lost, its meaning lost, unless you approach it as much through love as through hate." Instead of seeing life in terms of black or white—yes or no, no or yes—he has decided to try to embrace it all. "Diversity is the word," he says, not striving "toward colorlessness," but understanding that "America is woven of many strands," that "our fate is to become one, and yet many."

This, in fact, echoes Ellison's own views. With *Invisible Man,* he once explained, he hoped to fashion a story "as a raft of hope, perception and entertainment that might help keep us afloat as we tried to negotiate the snags and whirlpools that mark our nation's vacillating course toward and away from the democratic ideal."

 *By turns realistic, fable-like, and hauntingly surreal,* INVISIBLE MAN *is a visionary meditation on race and the multicultural heritage of the United States.*

AS I LAY DYING

(1930)

William Faulkner

The monologue delivered by Addie Bundren, the heroine of William Faulkner's groundbreaking 1930 novel, is a painful soliloquy about the isolation and meaninglessness of existence and the inadequacy of words to convey what she has experienced of marriage and motherhood. She now understands what her father meant when he said that "the reason for living is getting ready to stay dead," she says, and asserts that she has also learned "that words are no good; that words dont ever fit even what they are trying to say at."

Addie is only one of fifteen narrators in *As I Lay Dying,* which cuts between the points of view of different members of the Bundren family and their neighbors as they prepare to honor her request to be buried in her hometown and take her casket on an arduous forty-mile journey across rural Mississippi—a journey that itself becomes a metaphor for the road of life.

At the time of the book's publication, the fragmented structure of *As I Lay Dying* was regarded as highly experimental—a radical technique informed by Faulkner's exposure to the stream-of-consciousness techniques pioneered by Virginia Woolf and James Joyce and, some scholars have surmised, his fascination with the cubist art he glimpsed during a 1925 trip to Europe. His assimilation of those ideas in *As I Lay Dying* would form a narrative template (much like Akira Kurosawa's iconic 1950 film *Rashomon*) that has since inspired such disparate writers as Louise Erdrich, Marlon James, and David Mitchell and innovative television series like Showtime's *The Affair*.

Faulkner's collage-like narrative underscores the subjectivity of memory, the limitations of knowledge, the difficulty of understanding another individual's point of view. Addie is hardly the only character to feel isolated and bitter; through the stream-of-consciousness monologues of her four sons, her pregnant daughter, her sullen husband, and her assorted friends, we see the difficulties all of them have in connecting—the sense of aloneness and dislocation that, Faulkner suggests, is part of the human condition.

And yet the novel is not completely bleak. There is a darkly comic energy to the book and a sense that the characters recognize the absurdities of their journey—dragging Addie's decaying corpse through a flood and a fire to get her home—and yet persevere, despite their emotionally fraught relationships with her, out of a sense of loyalty and dedication. It's an attitude that captures Faulkner's frequently expressed belief that humanity—as he said in his Nobel Prize speech—will both "endure and prevail."

THE NEAPOLITAN QUARTET

MY BRILLIANT FRIEND (2012)

THE STORY OF A NEW NAME (2013)

THOSE WHO LEAVE AND THOSE WHO STAY (2014)

THE STORY OF THE LOST CHILD (2015)

Elena Ferrante
Translated by Ann Goldstein

Elena Ferrante's stunning Neapolitan quartet creates an indelible portrait of two women who are best friends and bitter rivals, cheerleaders of each other's literary ambitions and envious competitors for recognition. In the course of four novels (*My Brilliant Friend, The Story of a New Name, Those Who Leave and Those Who Stay, The Story of the Lost Child*) that span six decades, Elena and Lila become an unforgettable pair who take their place in our collective imagination as a matched set, along with Thelma and Louise, Laverne and Shirley, Arya and Sansa.

The two grew up together in a poor, violent, crime-ridden neighborhood in post–World War II Naples. Elena was the good girl, the hardworking, conscientious one, lucky enough to win a place at a decent school and to escape to a new life in Florence; she becomes a successful author and marries a professor from a prominent family. Lila was the fierce, impulsive, erratic one— a "terrible, dazzling girl" who is effortlessly brilliant and who intimidates everyone with her sharp elbows and sharper tongue.

She leaves school, marries young, and starts a successful business; although she becomes a kind of local power broker in their old neighborhood, she remains trapped there, her radiant artistic gifts unrealized.

The idea of tracing the stories of two women over the long arc of their lives is not exactly new; Arnold Bennett (*The Old Wives' Tale*) and Richard Yates (*The Easter Parade*) both drew powerful portraits of two very different sisters in their respective novels. But Ferrante's Neapolitan quartet opens out into a portrait of a city and an era while at the same time excavating the psyches of its two heroines in raw and unsparing emotional detail.

We come to sympathize with Elena's struggles to balance the competing demands of her career, her children, and her lover, Nino, just as we come to identify with Lila's impatience with her self-conscious friend and her daily frustrations with the criminal and political corruption that swirls through their old neighborhood.

Ferrante (a pseudonym for a writer who has declined to reveal her identity) captures the day-to-day texture of women's lives in the second half of the twentieth century: their efforts to define and hold on to a sense of identity and independence in the face of endless, banal household tasks, looking after husbands or boyfriends, and tending to children. The difficulty, for those with artistic ambitions, of clearing mental space in the face of mundane worries about paying the rent and making supper; the often dizzying gap between fiercely held beliefs—about politics, philosophy, feminism—and the compromises of daily life.

The ever-fluctuating relationship between Elena and Lila remains at the center of all four novels. Lila tends to be the aggressor, bullying Elena, making her feel guilty about not spending more time with her children and leaving her husband to run off with Nino (who, long ago, had been Lila's lover). She is a troublemaker and pot stirrer, but if Lila is often manipulative and undermining, she can also be generous and devoted. She takes care of Elena's daughters when Elena leaves on book tours, and she takes Elena's ailing mother (a matriarch as cruel and cunning as Tony Soprano's monstrous mother, Livia) to the hospital when she collapses.

We see Lila through Elena's eyes in these books, but at the same time Ferrante gives us an uncompromising portrait of Elena: her annoying need to feel that she's surpassed her childhood friend, whose brilliance she has always envied; her selfishness in placing her writing career and her passion for Nino before the needs of her children; her almost mercenary willingness to turn Lila's life into material for her books.

Over the years, as age and success and misfortune take their toll, the relationship between Lila and Elena shifts and mutates and yet, in many respects, remains the same. While Elena carefully notes their respective ups and downs—almost as if, she thinks, "an evil spell" meant "the joy or sorrow of one required the sorrow or joy of the other"—Lila points out there is "nothing to win" in the world, that "her life was full of varied and foolish adventures as much as mine, and that time simply slipped away without any meaning, and it was good just to see each other every so often to hear the mad sound of the brain of one echo in the mad sound of the brain of the other."

BOOKS BY DAVID FINKEL

THE GOOD SOLDIERS (2009)

THANK YOU FOR YOUR SERVICE (2013)

As the war on terror—"the longest war," "the forever war," "our children's children's war"—grinds on, it has already produced an outpouring of impressive writing, including Phil Klay's affecting and prismatic collection of stories *Redeployment,* Dexter Filkins's searing nonfiction account *The Forever War,* and Ben Fountain's poignant novel *Billy Lynn's Long Halftime Walk.*

Two of the most heart-stopping books about the war are *The Good Soldiers* and *Thank You for Your Service* by *The Washington Post*'s David Finkel, who chronicled the experiences of men from the Second Battalion, Sixteenth Infantry Regiment during a grueling tour in Iraq and their difficult journey home. The books are powered by those soldiers' own candor and eloquence, and they show the fallout that the decision to invade Iraq and the war's "ruinous beginnings" would have on a group of soldiers who, by various twists of fate, found themselves stationed in a hot spot on the edge of Baghdad. They are in a godforsaken place named Forward Operating Base Rustamiyah, a place that was "the color of dirt," where nearby streets had names like Route Pluto, Dead Girl Road, and Route Predators, the last of which "was constantly being seeded with hidden bombs."

Like Michael Herr's *Dispatches* and Tim O'Brien's *The Things They Carried,* Finkel's books capture the visceral experience of war—the fear, anticipation, violence, horror, and occasional moments of humanity that soldiers witness firsthand, day by day, minute by minute, and the slideshows of terrible pictures that will continue to run through their memories long after they have returned home.

We meet these young soldiers—whose average age is nineteen—strapping on sixty-plus pounds of armor and weaponry for their daily patrols, driving down roads riddled with IEDs, and searching for insurgents in buildings that could hide snipers and booby traps.

Finkel's books capture the visceral experience of war—the fear, anticipation, violence, horror, and occasional moments of humanity that soldiers witness firsthand, day by day, minute by minute.

Among the men Finkel introduces us to is the battalion's leader, Lieutenant Colonel Ralph Kauzlarich, "a skinny boy with jutting ears who had methodically re-created himself into a man who did the most push-ups, ran the fastest mile, and regarded life as a daily act of will"—a relentless optimist who believed his men would "be the difference" in winning the war and whom his men called "the Lost Kauz."

Another soldier we meet through Finkel is Adam Schumann, who, during the initial invasion, thought he had "a front seat to the greatest movie I've ever seen." He became a great soldier—

the "smart, decent, honorable" one who insisted "on being in the right front seat of the lead Humvee on every mission." But, Finkel reports, Schumann came home broken—unable to forget all the death and loss, unable to stop remembering his friend Sergeant First Class James Doster "being shredded" by a roadside bomb "on a mission Adam was supposed to have been on, too."

Tausolo Aieti of American Samoa, who at twenty-six has done three deployments, similarly cannot get past the day that the Humvee carrying him and three comrades was hit by a bomb. He never dreams about the two soldiers he saved. He dreams only about the one, James Harrelson, he failed to pull from the burning vehicle: "Harrelson, on fire, asking him, 'Why didn't you save me?'"

Finkel captures the sense of comradeship the men develop among themselves, and the difficulty they have, upon their return home, navigating the bureaucracy of the Veterans Affairs Department in an effort to get treatment for their wounds and post-traumatic stress disorder. He also chronicles their families' efforts to recover some facsimile of normalcy—or, in the words of one veteran's wife, to "come up with reasonable expectations of what can be," given their lingering physical and psychological wounds.

These two books are shattering and unforgettable contributions to the literature of war.

BOOKS ABOUT 9/11
AND THE WAR ON TERROR

THE LOOMING TOWER: Al-Qaeda and the Road to 9/11 (2006)
Lawrence Wright

THE FOREVER WAR (2008)
Dexter Filkins

*ANATOMY OF TERROR: From the Death of Bin Laden
to the Rise of the Islamic State* (2017)
Ali Soufan

Since 9/11, there has been an outpouring of books about the war on terror—about al-Qaeda and ISIS, about the wars America fought in Afghanistan and Iraq, about the fallout of those wars on soldiers, civilians, the United States, and the Middle East.

Many books on these subjects are impressive—illuminating, insightful, and important in understanding what led up to that terrible Tuesday morning in September 2001 and what has followed in the years since. The following three books are among the ones I've most frequently given or recommended to friends interested in the subject.

B ased on more than five hundred interviews, *The Looming Tower* by the *New Yorker* writer Lawrence Wright provides a searing look at the tragic events of 9/11 while situating them within a larger political and cultural framework. By focusing on the lives and careers of several key players, Wright has written a propulsive and highly immediate account that reminds us how the political and the personal are often braided together.

Wright's book suggests that "the charisma and vision of a few individuals shaped the nature" of the contest between Islam and the West. While "the tectonic plates of history were certainly shifting," promoting a period of conflict between those two cultures, he argues, the emergence of al-Qaeda "depended on a unique conjunction of personalities"—most notably, Osama bin Laden, whose leadership "held together an organization that had been bankrupted and thrown into exile," and his deputy Ayman al-Zawahiri, who promoted the apocalyptic notion that only violence could change history.

The Looming Tower also suggests that the events of September 11 were not inevitable. Rather, bad luck, the confluence of particular decisions and chance encounters, and dithering on the part of U.S. officials all contributed to al-Qaeda's success in pulling off its nefarious plans that sunny September day.

Intercut with the portraits of bin Laden and Zawahiri are equally compelling ones of the flamboyant FBI counterterrorism chief John O'Neill (who died on 9/11, having left the bureau to become chief of security for the World Trade Center) and a small band of dedicated FBI and CIA operatives, who for years had worried about al-Qaeda and who, in the months before 9/11, worked furiously, in the face of bureaucratic complacency and infighting, to head off a probable attack.

Dexter Filkins's book *The Forever War*—based on his coverage of the wars in Iraq and Afghanistan for *The New York Times*—captures the war on the ground with uncommon eloquence and insight. It's a harrowing and urgent book that combines a reporter's legwork and sense of historical context with a tactile, novelistic understanding of the human sorrow and unbearableness of war. It gives us indelible snapshots of the young American soldiers who fought there and the Iraqis who knew they would have to go on living there long after the Americans had left.

Filkins describes the momentary hope, when hundreds of Iraqis, dressed in their best clothes, crowded into the Fallujah Youth Center to attend an American-style caucus to choose representatives for the provincial councils, and he describes how the city soon became a stronghold of the insurgency, and would be left decimated by U.S.-led efforts to retake the city. He describes the incessant car bombings, the desperate civilians targeted by the insurgents, the wreckage of homes and entire neighborhoods by American bombings, the razor wire and blast walls people put up for protection, the lies told by Iraqi and American politicians.

He introduces us to Khalid Hassan, a young Palestinian Iraqi who worked for the *Times* in Baghdad and who was shot and killed one day by a group of gunmen who pulled alongside his car; and Fakhri al-Qaisi, a Baghdad dentist, who was targeted by a Shiite death squad for being a Sunni fundamentalist, mistrusted by Sunni insurgents for being willing to deal with the Americans, and questioned by the Americans for having links to the insurgency.

When he was in Iraq, Filkins wrote, he "might as well have been circling the earth from a space capsule, circling in farthest orbit.

Like Laika in Sputnik. A dog in space. Sending signals back to base, unmoored and weightless and no longer keeping time. Home was far away, a distant place that gobbled up whatever I sent back, ignorant and happy but touchingly hungry to know."

Leaving was just as hard, having "become part of the place, part of the despair, part of the death and the bad food and the heat and the sandy-colored brown of it."

I n *Anatomy of Terror,* the former FBI special agent Ali Soufan compares al-Qaeda to its vicious spin-off, the Islamic State, and draws an analogy between those terrorist organizations and the mythical Hydra: cut off one head and two more quickly sprout.

Soufan—who plays a pivotal role in Lawrence Wright's book *The Looming Tower*—writes with immense knowledge and on-the-ground experience hunting down and interrogating terrorists. He was a supervisor of counterterrorism operations and the investigation of events surrounding 9/11 and was instrumental in identifying the September 11 hijackers and Khalid Sheikh Mohammed as the architect of those attacks. Soufan extracted crucial information not through torture but by building a rapport with his subjects, sparring with them over interpretations of the Quran, and using old-fashioned logic and psychology. In fact, he became an outspoken critic of the Bush administration's so-called enhanced interrogation techniques, arguing that torture is morally wrong, un-American, and ineffective—generating false leads and unreliable information and helping terrorists find new recruits.

In *Anatomy of Terror*, Soufan provides a detailed portrait of al-Qaeda's bureaucratic operation, describing Osama bin Laden's penchant for micromanagement ("Please send me the résumés of all the brothers who might be nominated for high administrative positions now or in the future"). And he contrasts the different philosophies and divergent trajectories of al-Qaeda and the Islamic State, suggesting that the personalities of their leaders shaped the organizations. Of the relationship between the soft-spoken bin Laden and Abu Musab al-Zarqawi, the fiery militant who founded the group that would become the Islamic State, Soufan quotes an intelligence officer: it was a case of "loathing at first sight."

Soufan underscores the disastrous role that the U.S. invasion of Iraq and its bungled occupation played in fueling terrorism, creating chaos and a power vacuum in Iraq—the perfect incubator for insurgent violence and bloodshed. Two calamitous decisions made by the Americans—dissolving the Iraqi Army and banning members of Saddam Hussein's Baath Party from positions of authority—would prove particularly fateful.

Soufan gives us a keen sense of how these terrorist groups operate. He also maps the factors that lead individuals to become jihadis in the first place and the ways al-Qaeda and the Islamic State use publicity to recruit members and promote their brand.

"Know your enemy," Soufan quotes Sun Tzu, adding that empathy is a useful tool in this war—"not in the colloquial sense of sharing another person's perspective, but in the clinical sense of being able to see the world through another person's eyes." By understanding al-Qaeda and the Islamic State, he writes, we can better "combat the destructive ideology they represent."

THE GREAT GATSBY

(1925)

F. Scott Fitzgerald

L ike Vincent van Gogh's *Starry Night* and Leonardo da Vinci's *Mona Lisa, The Great Gatsby* suffers from overfamiliarity. Many of us had to write high school papers on Fitzgerald's novel, dissecting his use of symbols (the green light, the eyes of Doctor T. J. Eckleburg, the valley of ashes), and his views on class and status and money.

Worse, Baz Luhrmann's glossy 2013 movie adaptation felt like a two-hour-plus-long ad for designer labels like Prada and Tiffany and was accompanied by shameless merchandising that included promotions from Brooks Brothers, M.A.C. cosmetics, and even the Trump Hotel, which offered a special $14,999 package (including a three-night stay in a suite overlooking New York's Central Park, chauffeured car service, and a piece of Ivanka Trump jewelry).

Despite such marketing campaigns that willfully misconstrued Fitzgerald's intent, *Gatsby* has endured. Nearly a century after its publication, it remains one of the most emblematic distillations ever written about the promises—and disappointments—of the American dream. The slim novel is, at once, a gorgeously written prose poem about the sense of wonder that the "fresh, green breast of the new world" once incited in immigrants' minds and a devastating portrait of how that dream often became tarnished by greed and corruption and an inability to distinguish between "the

green light, the orgastic future" and the meretricious trinkets of success and evanescent riches.

Because we see Gatsby through the narrator Nick Carraway's eyes, we can appreciate both his "heightened sensitivity to the promises of life" and the folly of his belief that you can "repeat the past"; the innocence of his conviction that he could live up to "his Platonic conception of himself" and win back his dream girl, Daisy; and his fatal naïveté about people like the Buchanans who "smashed up things and creatures and then retreated back into their money or their vast carelessness, or whatever it was that kept them together, and let other people clean up the mess they had made."

The Great Gatsby is an elegy to the Jazz Age and a wary but captivating portrait of Gotham in the 1920s, written in incandescent, painterly prose. But, at heart, it is a story about lost illusions—Nick's and Gatsby's, which in turn foreshadow the sense of emotional exhaustion that Fitzgerald would later chronicle in his autobiographical *Crack-Up* essays.

Fitzgerald wrote that Gatsby's dream was behind him, "somewhere back in that vast obscurity beyond the city, where the dark fields of the republic rolled on under the night."

Regarding his own "crack-up," Fitzgerald equated his nostalgia for his lost youth with the sense of disillusion and despair that the nation experienced as the boom years of the 1920s gave way to the Depression. "My own happiness in the past," he recalled, "often approached such an ecstasy that I could not share it even with the person dearest to me but had to walk it away in quiet streets and lanes with only fragments of it to distil into little lines in books."

GOULD'S BOOK OF FISH
A Novel in Twelve Fish

(2001)

Richard Flanagan

G ould's Book of Fish is a novel about fish the way *Moby-Dick*
is a novel about whales.
　　　Inspired by the biography of a nineteenth-century
thief and forger named William Buelow Gould—who created a
vibrant series of fish paintings while serving time in the notorious
Tasmanian prison on Sarah Island—Flanagan's novel gives us an
excruciating account of life in that penal colony, where almost
everyone meets a bloody and terrible end. At the same time, this
dazzling, phantasmagorical novel opens out into a dazzling
philosophical meditation on art and nature and history, on human
suffering and transcendence, on the devastating consequences
of British colonialism and Enlightenment-age hubris and the "age
of abominations" in which genocidal massacres were carried out
against Australia's Aborigines.

Gould's Book of Fish is an audacious and thoroughly original
novel, even as it triggers dominoes of associations in the reader's
mind: among others, Melville, Joyce, and García Márquez; Rabelais
and Swift; Henry Fielding and Laurence Sterne; Pieter Brueghel
and Hieronymus Bosch. As Flanagan tells it, Gould's fish paintings
were meant to encapsulate all that the artist knew and loved
and feared, and in these pages Flanagan does something similar,

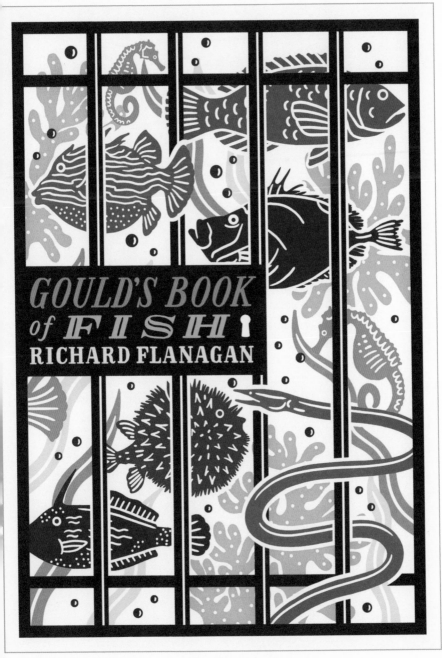

GOULD'S BOOK of FISH

RICHARD FLANAGAN

 *As told by Flanagan, Gould's story is as harrowing as* PAPILLON, *Henri Charrière's famous account of his incarceration in the prison camp on Devil's Island, and as inventive as one of Jorge Luis Borges's Möbius-strip-like tales.*

using the magic of words to conjure up the myriad worlds Gould traversed before he ended up in prison, and the imaginary ones he created in his head. There are all manner of amazements here, both horrifying and beautiful, including a murderous pig, a talking head, a pink marble palace rising from the South Pacific sands, and a flock of sulphur-crested cockatoos "painted to resemble baby macaws & trained to recite melancholic verse in the manner of Pope."

Flanagan's Gould—described as a "sloe-souled, green-eyed, gap-toothed, shaggy-haired & grizzle-gutted" convict—is awaiting execution in a fetid cell that fills with water every day when the tide comes in. He proves to be an entertaining if highly unreliable narrator, recounting his early adventures in England and America, where he claims to have studied painting with a man named Audubon. In a meandering, word-drunk narrative, he recalls how he wandered "hither & thither, at first in search of gold & glory, & then in search of an explanation" of his life, and how, as a prisoner on Sarah Island, he decided to reinvent himself as an artist.

He realizes that creating phony Constables for his jailer (who sells them for large sums of money) and doing portraits of the prison's commandant are means of escaping far more onerous duties. The demented commandant, who dreams of bringing European grandeur to the desolate prison island, orders Gould to paint scenic backdrops for a railway to nowhere that will be built with slave labor. Meanwhile, the prison doctor, who dreams of scientific recognition, enlists Gould's help in creating an encyclopedic survey of Tasmania's fish—a project that Gould invests with his love for nature's ingenuity and his own yearning for freedom.

As told by Flanagan, Gould's story is as harrowing as *Papillon*, Henri Charrière's famous account of his incarceration in the prison camp on Devil's Island, and as inventive as one of Jorge Luis Borges's Möbius-strip-like tales. The novel is filled with horrifying accounts of the torture and privations suffered by Gould and his fellow inmates, and yet in the face of this Hobbesian world of "endless labour, ceaseless brutality & pointless violence" it also radiates an appreciation for "the marvelous, the extraordinary, the gorgeously inexplicable wonder of a universe," and a faith in the human imagination's ability to alchemize suffering into art.

THE LETTERS OF GUSTAVE
FLAUBERT, 1830–1857

(1980)

Selected, Edited, and Translated by Francis Steegmuller

>>> ❂ <<<

laubert's doctrine of impersonality in art is well-known: "An author in his book must be like God in the universe, present everywhere and visible nowhere." But if his finely hammered, painstakingly crafted fiction showcased Flaubert's austere aesthetic theories, his letters were as intimate, funny, profane, and self-pitying as anything written by a twenty-first-century blogger, and at the same time they provide a remarkable window into the novelist's creative process and the writing of his masterpiece, *Madame Bovary*.

Since childhood, Flaubert had a single-minded determination to become a writer: by the age of ten, he had ideas for thirty different plays; as a teenager, he wrote an ambitious story about Satan; and as a young man, he settled into a hermit-like existence at his parents' house in the provincial village of Croisset, writing (or agonizing about writing) up to eighteen hours a day.

He complained that he'd spent a week writing a single page and three days making two corrections. He talked about the difficulty of walking a tightrope balanced above "the two abysses of lyricism and vulgarity." And he warned other authors that writing was not therapeutic: "Do not imagine you can exorcise what oppresses you in life by giving vent to it in art. No. The heart's dross does not find its way on to paper: all you pour out there is ink."

Often, Flaubert used animal metaphors to convey his laborious efforts to write. He proclaimed he'd been "working like a mule for fifteen long years" in an effort to produce one good book; bellowing "like a gorilla" when he read his own sentences out loud to himself; and spending days in quiet introspection, living "like a dreamy oyster," in "fishlike silence."

Flaubert's letters are filled with his thoughts about literature, philosophy, and creativity, along with plenty of narcissistic asides about his moods and his health (at thirty-two, he said, "I am aging: there go the teeth, and soon I shall be quite hairless"). His lover Louise Colet, whom he would see only once every two or so months, understandably complained that "in his letters, Gustave never speaks to me of anything except art—or himself."

While Colet was constantly imploring him to spend more time with her, Flaubert would respond with exasperated advice to read or work more, or he would explain why he couldn't be a more attentive companion. He was too steeped in solitude, too "racked by doubts from within and without," to be "the man for you to love. I love you as best I can; badly, not enough, I know it. I know it, oh God!"

He did write to her often and at great length, and his letters to her form an extraordinary chronicle of his creation of *Madame Bovary*—how he envisioned the novel, how he researched it and tried to imagine his way into his characters' lives, and how he laboriously revised and rewrote. For this alone, Flaubert's letters—expertly translated and edited by the scholar Francis Steegmuller—make for fascinating reading for writers and lovers of books.

Books are made the same way pyramids are made, Flaubert wrote in one letter: "There's some long-pondered plan, and then great blocks of stone are placed one on top of the other, and it's back-breaking, sweaty, time-consuming work. And all to no purpose! It just stands like that in the desert! But it towers over it prodigiously."

SINATRA! THE SONG IS YOU
A Singer's Art

(1995)

Will Friedwald

His voice—*The* Voice—provided the soundtrack for generations of Americans as they navigated the rocky shoals of love and romance and heartbreak. It was the most famous voice in the world, bridging the decades from World War II to the waning years of the twentieth century, the voice that millions danced to and listened to on radios, jukeboxes, and hi-fi sets.

He was the tough guy with Bond-like savoir faire who sang with uncommon tenderness about loneliness and yearning. A ring-a-ding-ding Vegas showman who could articulate the existential solitude of the human condition with more conviction than any singer on the planet. Fans could recognize his voice from two or three perfectly phrased syllables, and they knew him instantly from his rakishly tilted hat, the coat slung over one shoulder, the Camels and Jack Daniel's. He was the original teen heartthrob and the harbinger of a new age of celebrity. When it snowed, one writer observed, "girls fought over his footprints, which some took home and stored in refrigerators."

Sinatra never wrote a memoir, but his best self is there in the hundreds of songs he recorded: the loneliness he felt as a child, the joy and buoyancy of youthful love and success, the heartbreak he experienced with the end of his marriage to Ava Gardner. "Sinatra only offers the undistilled emotions without commentary or anything like a moral lesson," the music critic Will Friedwald has written. He "offers no wisdom, only empathy."

For readers eager to learn more about Sinatra's music (for that matter, to learn more about art), there is no better book than Friedwald's *Sinatra! The Song Is You*—a revealing study of the singer's artistry, based on interviews with many of the musicians and arrangers he worked with over the years, and the author's own intimate familiarity with his oeuvre. Friedwald explicates the irreducible magic of such nonpareil albums as *Songs for Swingin' Lovers!* and *Only the Lonely* while reminding us just how groundbreaking such works were in the history of popular music. The sections about Sinatra's work with Nelson Riddle eloquently illuminate their collaboration, each man pushing "the other to heights neither could achieve individually," while the book as a whole attests to Sinatra's perfectionism and devotion to detail— not just his own phrasing and control of rhythm and tempo, but also his thoughtful choice of songs to sustain the mood of a given album, his selection of musicians to work with on individual tracks, and the last-minute adjustments he made to arrangements and orchestrations.

Sinatra's greatest gift lay in his talent for storytelling and his ability, like that of the most talented of Method actors, to put his own deepest emotions into his art. "Having lived a life of violent emotional contradictions, I have an over-acute capacity for sadness as well as elation," he once observed. "Whatever else has been said about me is unimportant: when I sing, I believe, I'm honest."

GABRIEL
GARCÍA MÁRQUEZ

ONE
HUNDRED
YEARS
OF
SOLITUDE

ONE HUNDRED YEARS
OF SOLITUDE

(1967; English translation, 1970)

Gabriel García Márquez
Translated by Gregory Rabassa

A flock of yellow butterflies that announces a man's appearance; a plague of insomnia and forgetfulness so extreme that people are forced to label everything with signs ("This is the cow. She must be milked every morning."); the miracle of ice, seen for the first time, in the South American jungle; a beautiful woman who ascends into the heavens along with the sheets hung out to dry on the laundry line; a goldsmith who obsessively makes tiny gold fish, which he then melts down so he can start over again; a rainstorm that lasts four years, eleven months, and two days; a mysterious manuscript that foretells a family's future—these are just some of the wondrous images that animate Gabriel García Márquez's stunning masterwork, *One Hundred Years of Solitude*.

The magus of magical realism, García Márquez used his inexhaustible imagination and exuberant sleight of hand to conjure the miraculous in his fiction—a testament to his belief in the permeable membrane between the extraordinary and the mundane, the familiar and the fantastic. In *One Hundred Years of Solitude*, he told the story of the fictional town of Macondo and seven generations of the Buendía family—a story that reads as a kind of mythologized history of Latin America and as a biblical epic about loss and change and the vicissitudes of life in a fallen world.

Magical realism flourished in places like Latin America, where wars and revolutions and dictators made for history that often felt surreal, beyond the grasp of more naturalistic storytelling techniques. In the case of García Márquez, his fascination with the phantasmagorical was as rooted in his own childhood and family history as it was in the civil wars and political upheavals of his native Colombia. The remote town of Aracataca, where he grew up, inspired the world of Macondo—a place where the boundaries between reality and dreams dissolve and blur together, as in a Fellini or Buñuel movie. García Márquez's grandfather painted the walls of his workshop white so that the imaginative boy would have an inviting surface on which to draw and fantasize, and his grandmother spoke of the visions she experienced every day— the rocking chair that rocked alone, "the scent of jasmines from the garden" that "was like an invisible ghost."

In the end, it's not politics but time and memory and love that stand at the heart of García Márquez's work. How the histories of nations and families often loop back on themselves, how time past shapes time present, how passion can alter the trajectory of a life— these are the melodies that thread their way through *Solitude* and the magical bookend to that novel, *Love in the Time of Cholera.*

Half a century after its publication, *Solitude* would become one of the most influential novels of all time—alchemizing the modernist innovations of Faulkner and Joyce and inspiring new generations of writers, from Toni Morrison to Salman Rushdie to Junot Díaz. It remains a book of "miracles and magic," mirrors and mirages, that transcends languages and cultures and attests to the breathtaking powers of the human imagination. García Márquez taught us to read in color.

THE IDEA FACTORY

Bell Labs and the Great Age of American Innovation

(2012)

Jon Gertner

I n today's world of Apple, Google, and Facebook, the name
might not ring any bells for most readers, but for decades—
from the 1920s through the 1980s—Bell Labs, the research
and development wing of AT&T, was the most innovative scientific
organization in the world. As the journalist Jon Gertner argues in
The Idea Factory, it was where the future was invented.

Bell Labs was behind many of the innovations that have come
to define modern life, including the transistor (the building block
of digital products), the laser, the silicon solar cell, and the
computer operating system called Unix (which would serve as the
basis for a host of other computer languages). Bell Labs developed
the first communications satellites, the first cellular telephone
systems, and the first fiber-optic cable systems.

The Bell Labs scientist Claude Elwood Shannon effectively
founded the field of information theory, which would revolutionize
thinking about communications; other Bell Labs researchers helped
push the boundaries of physics, chemistry, and mathematics while
defining new industrial processes like quality control.

Gertner introduces us to the scientists behind the phenomenal
success of Bell Labs and makes their discoveries and inventions
utterly comprehensible—indeed, thrilling—to the lay reader. He
deftly puts their work in the context of what was known at the

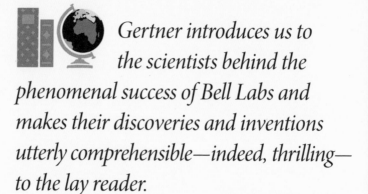

Gertner introduces us to the scientists behind the phenomenal success of Bell Labs and makes their discoveries and inventions utterly comprehensible—indeed, thrilling—to the lay reader.

time (and what would rapidly evolve from their initial discoveries in the decades since), even as he describes in remarkably lucid terms the steps by which one discovery led—sometimes by serendipity, sometimes by dogged work—to another, as well as the procedures by which ideas were turned by imaginative engineers into inventions and eventually into products that could be mass-produced.

At the same time, Gertner captures the electric, collegial atmosphere at the company's New Jersey campuses: a mixture of entrepreneurial zeal, academic inquiry, and a passion to achieve things that initially seemed technologically impossible. He suggests that the visionary leadership of the researcher-turned-executive Mervin Kelly played a large role in Bell Labs' sense of mission and its ability to institutionalize the process of innovation so effectively. Kelly believed that an "institute of creative technology" needed a critical mass of talented scientists—whom he initially housed in a single building where physicists, chemists, mathematicians, and engineers were encouraged to exchange ideas—and he gave his researchers the time to pursue their own investigations, "sometimes without concrete goals, for years on end."

That freedom, of course, was predicated on the steady stream of revenue provided (in the years before the AT&T monopoly was broken up in the early 1980s) by the monthly bills paid by telephone subscribers, which allowed Bell Labs to function "much like a national laboratory." Unlike, say, many tech companies today, which need to keep an eye on quarterly reports, Bell Labs in its heyday could patiently search out what Gertner calls "new and fundamental ideas" while using its immense engineering staff to "develop and perfect those ideas"—creating new products, then making them cheaper, more efficient, and more durable.

The very success of Bell Labs, Gertner notes, contained the seeds of its destruction. Not only was it producing too many ideas for a single company to handle, but some of its innovations (like the transistor) were so altering the technological landscape that its core business was being reduced to a mere part of the ever-expanding field of information and electronic technology—a field increasingly dominated by new rivals, with which a post-monopoly AT&T had difficulty competing.

In addition, as one Bell Labs researcher observed, the new business environment meant that "unfettered research" was no longer a logical or necessary investment for a company, which, in Gertner's words, "could profit merely by pursuing an incremental strategy rather than a game-changing discovery or invention."

THE PERIPHERAL

(2014)

William Gibson

William Gibson not only coined the word "cyberspace" back in 1982, but in his remarkable 1984 debut novel, *Neuromancer,* he foresaw the internet—"the consensual hallucination that was the matrix"—and the monumental impact it would have on how we think and connect.

His 2014 novel, *The Peripheral,* was just as uncannily clairvoyant, mapping two futures that feel ominously recognizable and real. That is one of Gibson's many gifts: an ability to imagine detailed worlds that are both strangely predictive windows into the future and haunting mirrors of our own times. Like Don DeLillo, he has an anthropologist's instinct for zeroing in on the surpassing strangeness of contemporary life, and he also possesses a shrewd understanding of how technological change drives social and cultural change.

The first future in *The Peripheral* transports us to a small American town somewhere in the South—a place where jobs, other than meth cooking and digital piracy, are scarce, big box stores and strip malls define the landscape, and surveillance and Homeland Security ("Homes") are omnipresent. Gibson's resourceful heroine, Flynne Fisher, a talented gamer (tag: "Easy Ice"), now works at a 3-D printing store. Her brother Burton, a veteran recovering from PTSD, has been supplementing his meager disability payments by working for a mysterious digital firm.

Gibson's second future takes us to an eerily depopulated, "post-jackpot" London in the early twenty-second century. This future, too, is unnervingly familiar to readers, circa 2020. This city-state is a kleptocracy, run by corporations, neo-monarchists, and Russian oligarchs; reality TV has merged with politics, and only the very rich have thrived.

The "jackpot," we learn, was a kind of slow-motion apocalypse that wiped out 80 percent of the population: "No comets crashing, nothing you could really call a nuclear war. Just everything else, tangled in the changing climate: droughts, water shortages, crop failures . . . every last alpha predator gone, antibiotics doing even less than they already did, diseases that were never quite the one big pandemic but big enough to be historic events in themselves."

When Flynne fills in for her brother (who is apparently testing a beta version of a game), she witnesses the gruesome murder of a woman that seems to have taken place not only online but in real life—in post-jackpot London. What ensues is a noirish, Borgesian detective story that crisscrosses time zones and decades and features "peripherals"—cyborg-like avatars that enable users to move through time.

The peripherals, the high-tech drones, the nanotechnology—all these are vividly rendered. But the interface in Gibson's stories between the real and the virtual worlds, between the human and the machine, is always about more than the hardware. It's also about how technology—data, information, misinformation, algorithms—alters people's daily lives and their apprehension of themselves, how data retrieval and artificial intelligence refashion our sense of history and create both nostalgia and a sense of loss, how science can open new horizons for human beings and at the same time remind them of their mortality and limitations.

THE EXAMINED LIFE
How We Lose and Find Ourselves

(2013)

Stephen Grosz

Freud's famous case studies, like Dora, the Wolf Man, Little Hans, and the Rat Man, are psychoanalytic readings, suspenseful detective stories, and elliptical narratives that possess all the drama and contradictions of modernist fiction. Not only is Freud a powerful writer, but his methodology and insights also have a lot in common with literary criticism and novelistic architecture. His patient portraits showcase his skills both as a critic, intent on deconstructing his subjects' lives, and as a masterly storyteller, adept at using unreliable narrators to explore the mysteries of love and sex and death. It's no coincidence that he liked to write about characters from Shakespeare, Goethe, Ibsen, and Sophocles (yes, Oedipus!), or that he paid so much attention to the language and imagery employed by his patients.

The Examined Life, by the psychoanalyst Stephen Grosz—who teaches at the Institute of Psychoanalysis and in the Psychoanalysis Unit at University College London—shares the best literary qualities of Freud's most persuasive work. The book distills the author's twenty-five years of work as a psychoanalyst into a series of slim, piercing chapters that read like a combination of Chekhov and Oliver Sacks. Grosz eloquently conveys the complexities of the process of psychoanalysis, inviting us to identify with his patients and their losses and regrets, even as we are made to marvel at the convolutions of the human mind.

Grosz quotes Isak Dinesen, who observed that "all sorrows can be borne if you put them into a story or tell a story about them," and he goes on to argue that stories can help us to make sense of our lives but that if "we cannot find a way of telling our story, our story tells us—we dream these stories, we develop symptoms, or we find ourselves acting in ways we don't understand."

Like Freud, Grosz is fond of literary allusions, and he's nimble at excavating the psychological subtext of literary classics. He reads Dickens's *Christmas Carol* as "a story about an extraordinary psychological transformation." One of the lessons it teaches, he argues, is that "Scrooge can't redo his past, nor can he be certain of the future"; he realizes change can take place only in the here and now. This is important, Grosz adds, because trying to change the past can leave us feeling helpless and depressed.

It's an observation that echoes Kierkegaard's definition of "the unhappiest man" as someone incapable of living in the present, dwelling instead in past memory or future hope.

Grosz writes with enormous empathy for his patients, gently encouraging them to recognize patterns in their lives while hearing out their own concerns. He reassures one patient that he will face all her problems with her, and he promises a seriously ill patient that he will visit him in the hospital for his regular sessions, five times a week. Being a psychoanalyst, Grosz writes, means spending his workdays "alone with another person, thinking—trying to be present." He is a "tour guide—part detective, part translator"— an editor who helps his patients connect the dots of their stories, helping them to make sense of their lives or, at the very least, assuring them that they are "alive in the mind of another."

SEABISCUIT
An American Legend

(1999)

Laura Hillenbrand

W hen I was growing up, there wasn't anything called Young Adult or YA reading. Instead, the books I searched for at the local library were Nancy Drew mysteries (I could spot one of those yellow covers from across the room), L. Frank Baum's *Oz* books, and animal stories like Joy Adamson's *Born Free* and *Living Free* and Sheila Burnford's *Incredible Journey,* about three pets who walk hundreds of miles across the Canadian wilderness to get home.

The Last Will and Testament of an Extremely Distinguished Dog was the first thing I read by Eugene O'Neill. *The Red Pony,* the first work I read by Steinbeck.

What I loved most of all, from the age of six or so, were horse books: Enid Bagnold's *National Velvet,* Walter Farley's endless series of *Black Stallion* novels, and anything by Marguerite Henry (and illustrated by Wesley Dennis)—like *Misty of Chincoteague, King of the Wind,* and *Brighty of the Grand Canyon.* All of which made me the ideal reader of Laura Hillenbrand's 1999 book, *Seabiscuit.*

If it's hard to understand why any but the most devoted fan of animal books would want to read a four-hundred-odd page book about a horse, it should be pointed out that Seabiscuit was no ordinary horse: as many as forty million fans would tune in to weekly radio broadcasts of his races, and in 1938 he reportedly received more newspaper coverage than Roosevelt, Hitler, or Mussolini. His match that year with his archrival, War Admiral—which pitted racing fans from the West Coast against racing fans from the East—was one of the decade's biggest sports events. And Hillenbrand uses Seabiscuit's story to create a sharply observed portrait of a Depression-era America bent on escapism and the burgeoning phenomenon of mass-media-marketed celebrity—a slice of history with some telling echoes of our own times.

Mostly, though, *Seabiscuit* just makes for terrific storytelling in the tradition of the animal stories I loved as a kid, and in the tradition of classic sports reporting that communicates, in the words of Jim McKay on ABC's *Wide World of Sports,* "the thrill of victory and the agony of defeat."

Seabiscuit emerges as the epitome of the underdog—a boxy, stubby-legged horse with a chronic weight problem and the amiable personality of a large, friendly dog—who ends up beating the sleek, high-strung Triple Crown winner War Admiral with ease. His victory in the "Race of the Century" is celebrated as a win for the West Coast over the East Coast; the blue-collar, working-class fans over the blue-blooded elite.

Hillenbrand's portraits of Seabiscuit's human companions are equally well drawn. There's his trainer Tom Smith, a former mustang wrangler; his owner Charles Howard, a self-made magnate who had found his calling selling Buicks; and his jockey Johnny "Red" Pollard, a scrappy veteran of the lawless bush tracks.

After he retired in 1940, tens of thousands of fans went to visit Seabiscuit at Howard's ranch some 150 miles north of San Francisco, where he sired more than a hundred foals and grew fat and "blissfully happy." An ending as happy as, if not happier than, those in all the animal books I loved as a child.

THE PARANOID STYLE IN AMERICAN POLITICS

(1964)

Richard Hofstadter

More than half a century after it was published, the historian Richard Hofstadter's *Paranoid Style in American Politics* reads like a description of the politics of fear and grievance promoted by Donald J. Trump.

Hofstadter defined "the paranoid style" as an outlook characterized by "qualities of heated exaggeration, suspiciousness, and conspiratorial fantasy" and focused on perceived threats to "a nation, a culture, a way of life." Its language is apocalyptic; its point of view, extremist. It regards its opponents as evil and ubiquitous while portraying itself as "manning the barricades of civilization."

Hofstadter noted that "the paranoid style" was not a new phenomenon. The anti-Catholic, anti-immigrant Know-Nothing Party reached its height in 1855, with forty-three members of Congress openly avowing their allegiance, but its power soon began to dissipate, after the party split along sectional lines. The toxic attitude would erupt again: most notably, during the 1950s with the anticommunist hysteria led by Senator Joseph McCarthy and in the 1960s with the emergence on the national stage of Governor George C. Wallace, who ran a presidential campaign fueled by racism and white working-class anger.

Early exemplars of "the paranoid style" like the anti-Catholic

movement, Hofstadter argued, often assumed a defensive stance—
fending off perceived "threats to a still established way of life." In
contrast, he wrote, the contemporary right wing tends to represent
segments of the population that already feel marginalized: "America
has been largely taken away from them and their kind, though
they are determined to try to repossess it"; they feel that "the old
American virtues have already been eaten away by cosmopolitans
and intellectuals."

Hofstadter's words uncannily anticipate the birth of the Tea Party
movement and the populist, anti-immigrant nativism inflamed
and exploited by Donald Trump. Economic anxieties exacerbated
by the 2008 financial crisis, along with the dislocations of rapid
social changes—wrought by technology, globalization, and shifting
demographics—have fueled a renewed sense of dispossession and
resentment. At the same time, Trump's attacks on "the deep state"
and the press replicate the anti-elitism Hofstadter diagnosed as
resentment against establishment figures like Franklin D. Roosevelt.

Among Hofstadter's other farsighted observations is this:
he writes that a "persistent psychic complex"—which a historian had
found among early millennial sects in Europe—corresponded to his
own findings about "the paranoid style," namely, "the megalomaniac
view of oneself as the Elect, wholly good, abominably persecuted,
yet assured of ultimate triumph; the attribution of gigantic and
demonic powers to the adversary; the refusal to accept the ineluctable
limitations and imperfections of human existence, such as transience,
dissention, conflict, fallibility whether intellectual or moral; the
obsession with inerrable prophecies." Sound familiar?

One of the few cheering thoughts in Hofstadter's classic book:
his observation that movements employing "the paranoid style"
tend to "come in successive episodic waves" that rise and crest,
but then recede (at least until their next incarnation).

THE ODYSSEY

Homer
Translated by Emily Wilson (2017)

Homer's *Odyssey* remains one of Western literature's great
urtexts, and it continues to inform our storytelling in
obvious and more sub-rosa ways. The story of Odysseus's
ten-year voyage home after the Trojan War is the archetypal hero's
journey, and it would be recapitulated in countless classics, from
The Lord of the Rings to *Star Wars* and Kubrick's *2001: A Space
Odyssey* to many Marvel comics action-adventure extravaganzas.
The Odyssey has also served as a template for a startling array of
literary works, including Joyce's *Ulysses,* Derek Walcott's *Omeros,*
and Charles Frazier's *Cold Mountain.*

The dangers of pride, the protean nature of identity, the tug-
of-war between fate and free will, the relationship between fathers
and sons—these eternal themes have all been framed by *The
Odyssey.* And more controversial themes concerning the aftermath
of war and the consequences of imperialism are embedded in
Homer's classic too. As the scholar Emily Wilson points out in
the introduction to her brilliant new translation, the Polyphemus
episode—in which Odysseus arrives in the land of the Cyclops,
barges into an inhabitant's cave, and then tricks, blinds, and robs
his host—"can be read as an attempt to justify Greek exploitation of
non-Greek peoples."

Wilson, the first woman to translate Homer's poem into English,
gives us an *Odyssey* of extraordinary immediacy and nuance: the

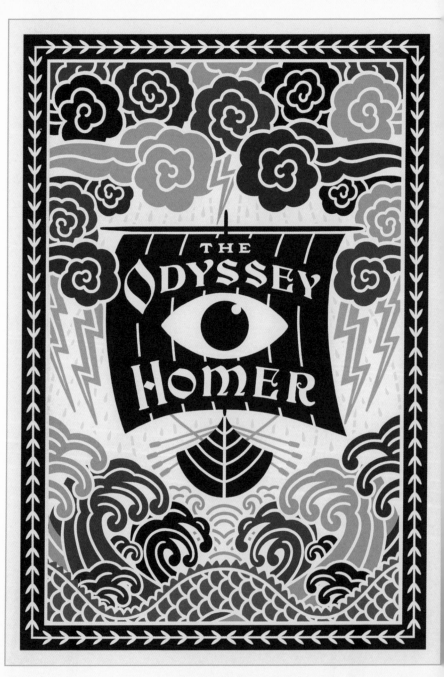

language is simple and direct, and the text leaves the modern reader with an appreciation of both the ambiguities of the story and the moral ambiguities of Odysseus as a hero.

There was always a troubling aspect to the "wily" war hero we knew from *The Odyssey* we studied in school—self-interested, manipulative, duplicitous. But in Wilson's translation, he emerges as an especially "complicated man," not merely a survivor of all manner of harrowing encounters with monsters and natural disasters, but also a "lying, self-interested sacker of cities." He is an adulterer with a double standard when it comes to women, but also a husband who chooses to return home to his wife, Penelope, instead of staying on with the nymph Calypso—a choice that implies an embrace of mortality over eternal life. He is a ruthless pirate, given to looking down on other cultures as ignorant and barbarous; a war hero who failed to bring his own men safely home and who oversaw the merciless slaughter not only of Penelope's suitors but also of the slave girls who slept with them, ordering his son Telemachus to "hack at them with long swords, eradicate / all life from them." As a narrator, he is self-dramatizing and decidedly unreliable (something Zachary Mason underscored in his inventive 2010 novel, *The Lost Books of "The Odyssey"*) as he spins the meaning of his own journey.

Wilson's astute introduction to this volume looks at the story through modern eyes while at the same time situating *The Odyssey* in context with the culture of its day. She points out that the text itself is "surprisingly clear-sighted" about its problematic hero—a text that "allows us to explore our desire for power and for permanence, in the world of imagination, while also showing us the darker side of these deep human dreams, hopes, and fears."

LAB GIRL

(2016)

Hope Jahren

Vladimir Nabokov once observed that "a writer should have the precision of a poet and the imagination of a scientist." The geobiologist Hope Jahren possesses both in spades. Her memoir, *Lab Girl,* is both a thrilling account of her discovery of her vocation and a gifted teacher's road map to the secret lives of plants—a book that, at its best, does for botany what Oliver Sacks's essays did for neurology, what Stephen Jay Gould's writings did for paleontology.

Jahren, a professor of geobiology, conveys the utter strangeness of plants: these machines, "invented more than 400 million years ago," that create sugar out of inorganic matter—wondrous machines upon which human life itself depends.

She describes the sound of plants growing in the Midwest: "At its peak, sweet corn grows a whole inch every single day, and as the layers of husk shift slightly to accommodate this expansion, you can hear it as a low continuous rustle if you stand inside the rows of a cornfield on a perfectly still August day."

She describes the miraculous ability of a cactus to sit, under a blazing desert sun, waiting years for rain: it sheds "its roots to prevent the parched soil from sucking all the water back out of it," then begins to contract, until its spines "form a dense and dangerous fur protecting what is now a hard, rootless ball of plant."

And she explains why the leaves at the top of a tree are smaller than those below, allowing "sunlight to be caught near the base whenever the wind blows and parts the upper branches."

By crosscutting between chapters about the life cycle of trees and flowers and other green things and chapters about her own coming of age as a scientist, Jahren underscores the similarities between humans and plants—tenacity, inventiveness, an ability to adapt—but, more emphatically, the radical otherness of plants: their dependence on sunshine, their inability to move or travel as we do, the redundancy and flexibility of their tissues ("a root can become a stem if need be, and vice versa").

Jahren's own childhood in a small Minnesota town, where there was snow on the ground nine months of the year, was filled with silences. Her great-grandparents had arrived there from Norway, and she writes that "vast emotional distances between the individual members of a Scandinavian family are forged early and reinforced daily." It was not unusual for her and her brothers "to go days without anything to say to each other."

Her sanctuary was the laboratory of her father, who taught introductory physics and earth science at a local community college. There she discovered the rituals and magic of science: she embraced its rules and procedures and the attention to detail it demanded. Science gave her what she needed: "a home as defined in the most literal sense, a safe place to be."

She communicates the electric excitement of discovering something new—something no one ever knew or definitively proved before—and the boring scientific grunt work involved in conducting studies and experiments: the days and weeks and months of watching and waiting and gathering data, the all-nighters, the repetitions, the detours, both serendipitous and unfruitful.

Jahren communicates the electric excitement of discovering something new—something no one ever knew or definitively proved before—and the boring scientific grunt work involved in conducting studies and experiments.

Along the way, she came to realize that her work as a scientist was also part of a larger enterprise. She was not like a plant but like an ant, "driven to find and carry single dead needles, one after the other, all the way across the forest and then add them one by one by one to a pile so massive that I can only fully imagine one small corner of it."

As a scientist, she goes on, she is indeed just an ant, "insufficient and anonymous, but stronger than I look and part of something that is much bigger than I am." She is part of the continuum of scientists who have built upon their predecessors' work and who will hand down their own advances to the next generation.

THE LIARS' CLUB

(1995)

Mary Karr

When she was eleven, Mary Karr wrote in her diary that when she grew up, she would "write one-half poetry and one-half autobiography." And this is exactly what she would end up doing. Her writing, both verse and prose, is raw, candid, and so precisely observed that it has the power to give readers an utterly visceral understanding of what she is writing about—be it the swampy East Texas town where she grew up (a town so small that its mayor's "only real job was to turn on the traffic light every morning"), her grandmother's rapacity for argument (she "just clamped down on it like a Gila monster"), or the delight she took in hanging out with her father and his friends as they regaled one another with stories (just being out with him and his buddies "lights me up enough for somebody to read by me").

Her 1995 memoir, *The Liars' Club,* is an astonishing book, which attests that Karr inherited her father's brilliant gift for storytelling and his ability to hold an audience's rapt attention. Funny, gritty, and unsparing, Karr possesses an utterly distinctive voice that's part badass Texas girl and part lyric poet, and in these pages she draws an indelible portrait of her family that possesses the emotional afterlife of a memorable novel and the shocking frisson of being true. No surprise that the book helped catalyze the memoir boom of the 1990s, pointing to the boundless possibilities of the genre and the enduring power of personal testimony.

Karr's mother, the former Charlie Marie Moore, grew up in the dust bowl of West Texas, married at the age of fifteen, and moved away to the glamorous city of New York, where she enrolled in art school. She would marry six more times, and after returning to Texas, she spent more and more time drinking and dreaming of her lost life in New York. She inhaled books by Sartre and Marx and wept when she listened to opera and jazz. In the parlance of East Texas, Karr writes, her mother was "nervous"—a term that "applied with equal accuracy to anything from chronic nail-biting to full-blown psychosis." During one fit of madness, Charlie Marie set fire to her daughters' toys and clothes and threatened them with a butcher knife.

Karr's father, Pete—who met Charlie Marie one night under a bright "General Electric" moon—was as steady and steadfast as her mother was erratic and moody. Pete was "the guy you set your watch by," a man who never missed a day of work in forty-two years and could take pleasure "in the small comforts—sugar in his coffee, getting the mockingbird in our chinaberry tree to answer his whistle."

The Karr household was eccentric to say the least. Their idea of dinner seems to have involved everyone sitting on an edge of her parents' bed, facing in different directions. As the years passed, the family gradually succumbed to the centrifugal force of its secrets, disappointments, and losses. After Charlie Marie moved her mother—a vituperative old woman who carried "an honest-to-God hacksaw" in her purse—into the house, Pete withdrew into his work and increasingly began "backpedaling out of the daddy business." Days often passed without his returning home to see Mary and her sister, Lecia.

Acts of violence and negligence proliferated. When she was seven, Karr was raped by a boy from school and later sexually molested by a babysitter. When her sister broke her collarbone in a horseback-riding accident, no one even volunteered to take her to a doctor. When her mother started drinking, Karr would hide her car keys to keep her off the roads, or pretend to talk on the phone to prevent her from bad-mouthing the neighbors.

The chaos taught Karr how to lock all her "scaredness down in my stomach until the fear hardens into something I hardly notice," and it taught her the writerly art of detachment. "God answered my prayers," she wrote, and "I learned to make us all into cartoons." One of the things that's remarkable about this book, however, is that Karr never turns her parents into two-dimensional stick figures. Instead, she writes about them with enormous empathy and compassion, making us see them as incredibly palpable human beings—flawed, unreliable, even treacherous, but also vulnerable and desperate to love.

The Liars' Club is a fierce and loving act of remembrance that redeems the past even as it recaptures it on paper.

A TESTAMENT OF
HOPE:
THE ESSENTIAL WRITINGS + SPEECHES OF MARTIN LUTHER KING, JR.

A TESTAMENT OF HOPE

The Essential Writings and Speeches of
Martin Luther King, Jr.

(1986)

Edited by James M. Washington

Martin Luther King, Jr.'s life was a testament to the power of one man to bend the arc of history toward justice. And more than half a century after his death, his speeches and writings not only stand as essential documents in the history of the American civil rights movement: they have inspired change—and continue to inspire change—around the world from eastern Europe to Soweto to Tiananmen Square to Hong Kong.

The son, grandson, and great-grandson of Baptist ministers, King grew up in the church, and the sonorous cadences and ringing, metaphor-rich language of the King James Bible came instinctively to him. Quotations from the Bible, along with its vivid imagery, animated his writings, and he used them to situate the painful history of African Americans within the context of Scripture.

In "Letter from Birmingham Jail," King referred to Saint Augustine and Saint Thomas Aquinas, in drawing a distinction between *just* and *unjust* laws. In "The Drum Major Instinct," he used a passage from Saint Mark as a springboard by which to argue that the human craving for recognition—the "desire to lead the parade"—must be put in the service of justice, of fighting for the less fortunate. And in his "I Have a Dream" speech, he alluded to a well-known passage from Galatians, speaking of "that day when all of God's children—black men and white men, Jews and Gentiles, Protestants and Catholics—will be able to join hands."

The "Dream" speech also contains echoes of Shakespeare ("this sweltering summer of the Negro's legitimate discontent") and popular songs like Woody Guthrie's "This Land Is Your Land" ("Let freedom ring from the mighty mountains of New York," "Let freedom ring from the curvaceous slopes of California"). Such references added amplification and depth of field to the speech and gave audiences touchstones that might resonate with their own lives.

King, who had a doctorate in theology and once contemplated a career in academia, was shaped by his childhood in his father's church and by his later studies of thinkers like Reinhold Niebuhr, Gandhi, and Hegel. Along the way, he developed a gift for synthesizing disparate ideas and motifs and making them his own—a gift that enabled him to address many different audiences at once while taking ideas that some might find radical at first and making them feel accessible and familiar.

By nestling his arguments within a historical continuum, King was able to lend them the authority of tradition and the weight of association. For some in his audience, the articulation of his dream for America would have evoked conscious or unconscious memories of Langston Hughes's call in a 1935 poem to "Let America be the dream the dreamers dreamed" and W. E. B. Du Bois's description of the "wonderful America, which the founding fathers dreamed." His final lines in the March on Washington speech came from a Negro spiritual reminding listeners of slaves' sustaining faith in the possibility of liberation: "Free at last! Free at last! Thank God Almighty, we are free at last!"

For those less familiar with African American music and literature, there were allusions with immediate, patriotic connotations. Much the way Lincoln redefined the founders' vision of America in his Gettysburg Address by invoking the Declaration of Independence, so King in his "Dream" speech and his "Letter from Birmingham Jail" makes references to the Declaration of Independence. Such deliberate echoes helped universalize the moral underpinnings of the civil rights movement and emphasized that its goals were only as revolutionary as the founding fathers' original vision of the United States. King's dream for America's "citizens of color" was no more, no less than the American dream of a country where "all men are created equal."

The March on Washington and King's "Dream" speech would play an important role in helping pass the 1964 Civil Rights Act, and the Selma to Montgomery march that he led in 1965 would provide momentum for the passage of the Voting Rights Act. Much had been achieved in just those two years, but there was a long road ahead in the fight for equality and freedom and justice, requiring "tireless efforts and persistent work"—because, as King reminded us in his Birmingham Jail letter, "human progress never rolls in on wheels of inevitability."

But King—much like Abraham Lincoln—saw the events he witnessed, the marches he led, and the speeches he gave over the course of his career as part of a longer continuum in history. As he said in the last speech he gave before he was assassinated in 1968, "I've seen the promised land. I may not get there with you. But I want you to know tonight, that we, as a people, will get to the Promised Land."

ON WRITING
A Memoir of the Craft

(2000)

Stephen King

This book not only belongs in every writing class in high school and college but should be read by anyone who has ever wanted to write a novel or short story.

A lot of writers first became aware of the power of storytelling—the power of the imagination to make other people feel wonder, fear, anticipation—when they were kids, reading novels (or seeing movies based on novels) by Stephen King. And in this slim, passionate volume, King lays out—in direct, personal terms—what he's learned about the craft of storytelling in the course of his own prodigious career.

His book is as useful as Strunk and White's classic *The Elements of Style*—and a lot more inspiring and fun. Its commonsense rules about writing are stated simply—like "letting go of fear and affectation" and stripping out unnecessary adverbs and pretentious words. It also provides encouraging advice for novice writers who agonize over "le mot juste" and struggle to come up with the right idea or the perfect plot twist.

Among King's observations:

- The writer's job, as he sees it, isn't to find great ideas "but to recognize them when they show up." Sometimes that means seizing upon a news story, which suggests an intriguing what-if premise. Sometimes that means putting two previously unrelated ideas together (as in King's first hit novel, *Carrie,* which added telekinesis to the theme of teenage bullying).

- Situations matter more than plot points. In many of his own books, King writes that he wanted "to put a group of characters (perhaps a pair; perhaps even just one) in some sort of predicament and then watch them work their way free."

- "Don't wait for the muse." Instead, King says, find a writing space with a door (but no telephone, no TV), settle on a daily writing goal, and stay put each day (every day) until that goal is met. Practice is essential.

- And, most important: "read a lot and write a lot." Regular reading, he says, "offers you a constantly growing knowledge of what has been done and what hasn't, what is trite and what is fresh, what works and what just lies there dying (or dead) on the page."

Few writers can come close to King's own daunting pace of ten pages—or two thousand words!—a day, which enables him to finish a first draft of a book in an astonishing three months. But his advice about pushing through a first draft is similar to the lesson learned by young reporters working on deadline: after you do all the legwork, quickly get something down on paper; you can then go back and fill in the holes, check facts, fine-tune the prose. Once a draft of the story exists, it can be edited, revised, rewritten, even taken apart and reassembled.

King's account of his own apprenticeship as a writer is as captivating as William Styron's fictionalized self-portrait in the opening chapters of *Sophie's Choice* or Philip Roth's portrait of his fictional alter ego Nathan Zuckerman's coming of age in *The*

Ghost Writer. King fills us in on some of the events that seem to have played a formative role in shaping his imagination (including being locked in a closet for hours by a cruel babysitter), and he chronicles his love of writing, which dates back to when he was six and wrote some stories about a group of magic animals, led by a large white bunny named Mr. Rabbit Trick. The stories delighted his mother and made her laugh and gave him an "immense feeling of possibility."

In 1999, King was walking down a road near his house in Maine and was hit by a van. The accident left him with a collapsed lung, four broken ribs, a fractured hip, and a lower leg broken in at least nine places. The pain in his hip was "just short of apocalyptic," but five weeks later he began to write again; in fact he went back to finish *On Writing*.

Some days, the writing was "a pretty grim slog," he remembers. But as his body began to heal and he settled back into a writing routine, he felt "that buzz of happiness, that sense of having found the right words and put them in a line. It's like lifting off in an airplane: you're on the ground, on the ground, on the ground . . . and then you're up, riding on a magical cushion of air and prince of all you survey. That makes me happy, because it's what I was made to do."

THE WOMAN WARRIOR
Memoirs of a Girlhood Among Ghosts

(1976)

Maxine Hong Kingston

In her stunning 1976 book, *The Woman Warrior,* Maxine Hong Kingston conjured up the ghosts of her Chinese family's past in poetic, white-hot prose. Mixing folktales and family legends, memories and dreams, the book provided a visceral sense of what it is to live within two cultures and to belong to neither, and what it was like to grow up with her mother's wildly contradictory teachings about the proper roles of women in society.

Kingston's mother, Brave Orchid, was a ferocious, larger-than-life matriarch, a "champion talker" and potent storyteller, a woman so intense that arguments with her would leave her daughter with "a spider headache" spreading out "in fine branches over my skull." Brave Orchid berates her daughter for being "Noisy. Talking like a duck. Disobedient. Messy" and says it will be difficult to find her a husband.

Women are traditionally meant to be wives or slaves, Brave Orchid warns, and tells her daughter a chilling story about her sister-in-law who committed adultery and bore the other man's child: her neighbors in the small Chinese village scorned and cursed her and vandalized her home; she ended up throwing herself and her baby into a well. Her family's reaction was just as terrible. "Don't tell anyone you had an aunt," Kingston's mother says. "Your father does not want to hear her name. She has never been born."

The brutal lesson: women must play by society's rules, and those who don't will be forgotten.

The shocking sexism of this tale stands in sharp contrast to other "talk-stories" told by Kingston's mother. One of Kingston's favorites was the story of Fa Mu Lan, a heroic woman who trained for years in the mountains, learning the way of the white tiger and the way of the dragon so that she could take her father's place in battle and avenge their besieged village; she is as fierce and dazzling a warrior as the brilliant martial arts fighters in *Crouching Tiger, Hidden Dragon* or the badass women in *Game of Thrones*.

And for all of Brave Orchid's recitations of ancient misogynist sayings, her own life was, in many ways, a testament to female independence. She was determined to become a doctor, and when she returned to her home village with a medical degree, she was "welcomed with garlands and cymbals." When she went "doctoring" in small villages, she would minister to the old and the sick and deliver babies in beds and pigsties. After she joined her husband in America in 1940, she gave birth to six children (all after the age of forty-five, she claimed) and worked in the family laundry.

Brave Orchid's stories are elliptical and contradictory, and in trying to sort out her family's history, Kingston uses her imagination to try to understand the experiences of her mother and her aunt—and to try to situate her own "American-normal" life in context with their lives and the myths she grew up on. The resulting book is as intense, surreal, and impassioned as Brave Orchid's stories. In fact, that is one of the things that connects mother and daughter, despite all their conflicts, confrontations, and cultural differences: both are virtuosic—and mesmerizing—storytellers.

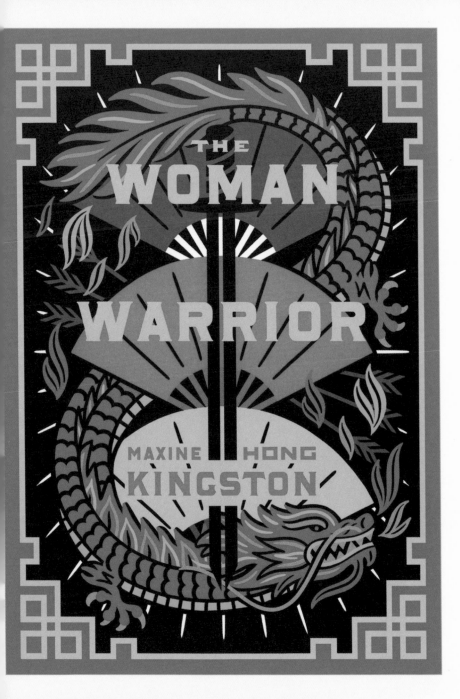

THE
WOMAN
WARRIOR

MAXINE HONG
KINGSTON

THE LANGUAGE OF
THE THIRD REICH

(1947; English translation, 2000)

Victor Klemperer
Translated by Martin Brady

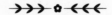

L anguage matters.

As Orwell observed in a well-known 1946 essay, language can "corrupt thought," and political language is often "designed to make lies sound truthful and murder respectable."

One of history's most detailed accounts of how totalitarianism infects everyday language was written by Victor Klemperer, a German-Jewish linguist who survived World War II in Dresden. Klemperer kept a remarkable set of diaries chronicling life under Nazi rule in Germany (*I Will Bear Witness*), and he also wrote a study, *The Language of the Third Reich,* about the Nazis' use of words as "tiny doses of arsenic" to poison and subvert German culture from within.

The book offers a harrowing account of how the Reich "permeated the flesh and blood of the people" through idioms, catchphrases, and sentence structures that were "imposed on them in a million repetitions and taken on board mechanically and unconsciously." It's also a cautionary tale, every bit as unnerving as Orwell's *1984,* about how swiftly and insidiously an autocrat can weaponize language to suppress critical thinking, inflame bigotry, and hijack democracy.

Klemperer didn't think Hitler compared with Mussolini as a speaker, and he was surprised that the Nazi leader—whom he saw as an angry, insecure man with a propensity to bellow—amassed such a following. He attributed Hitler's success less to his heinous ideology than to his skills at going around other politicians to reach out directly to the people, while portraying himself as their voice, their messiah. The big rallies that he and Goebbels staged were also a help. "The splendour of the banners, parades, garlands, fanfares and choruses" that surrounded Hitler's speeches, Klemperer noted, served as an effective "advertising ploy" that conflated the führer with the grandeur of the state.

As in the Soviet Union and Maoist China, words underwent a sinister metamorphosis in Nazi Germany. The word *fanatisch* (fanatical), Klemperer wrote, went from denoting "a threatening and repulsive quality" associated with bloodlust and cruelty to being an "inordinately complimentary epithet," evoking the qualities of devotion and courage needed to sustain the Reich. The word *kämpferisch* (aggressive, belligerent) also became a word of praise, meaning admirable "self-assertion through defense or attack." Meanwhile, the word *System* was scorned, because it was associated with the Weimar Republic and its institutions, which the Nazis despised in much the same way that some Trump followers today despise what they call "the deep state."

Hitler's *Mein Kampf* was published in 1925, and Klemperer argued that the book "literally fixed the essential features" of Nazi oratory and prose. In 1933, this "language of a clique became the language of the people." It would be as if, say, the argot of today's alt-right—its coded use of language to identify fellow travelers; its racist and misogynist slurs—were to be completely mainstreamed and made a part of routine political and social discourse.

Klemperer devoted an entire chapter to the Nazis' obsession with numbers and superlatives; everything had to be "the best" or "the most." If a German from the Third Reich went on an elephant hunt, Klemperer wrote, he would have to boast that he'd "finished off the biggest elephants in the world, in unimaginable numbers, with the best weapon on earth." Many of the Nazis' own numbers (regarding enemy soldiers killed, prisoners taken, audience numbers for a radio broadcast of a rally) were so exaggerated that they took on what Klemperer calls a "fairy-tale quality."

In 1942, Klemperer wrote, "Hitler says in the Reichstag that Napoleon fought in Russia in temperatures of minus 25 degrees, but that he, Commanding Officer Hitler, had fought at minus 45, even at minus 52."

The Nazis' lies, hyperbole, and hate-fueled rhetoric anatomized by Klemperer poisoned the language in Orwellian ways. "If someone replaces the words 'heroic' and 'virtuous' with 'fanatical' for long enough," Klemperer wrote, "he will come to believe that a fanatic really is a virtuous hero, and that no one can be a hero without fanaticism."

By making "language the servant of its dreadful system," he went on, the Third Reich procured it "as its most powerful, most public and most surreptitious means of advertising."

BOOKS ABOUT DEMOCRACY AND TYRANNY

ON TYRANNY: Twenty Lessons from the Twentieth Century (2017)
Timothy Snyder

HOW DEMOCRACIES DIE (2018)
Steven Levitsky and Daniel Ziblatt

THE ROAD TO UNFREEDOM: Russia, Europe, America (2018)
Timothy Snyder

Here are three lucid and succinct books by eminent scholars that explore how democracies fail and how authoritarians rise to power—topics of immediate concern today, given troubling developments around the world. Indeed, the watchdog group Freedom House reported in 2019 that global freedom had declined for the thirteenth consecutive year: antidemocratic leaders in countries like Hungary and Poland have undermined institutions that protect freedom of expression and the rule of law; Vladimir Putin's Russia has sabotaged democracy with repressive policies at home, and disinformation and election interference abroad; and in America, President Trump "has assailed essential institutions and traditions including the separation of powers, a free press, an independent judiciary, the impartial delivery of justice, safeguards against corruption, and most disturbingly, the legitimacy of elections."

"History does not repeat, but it does instruct," the historian Timothy Snyder wrote in his 2017 bestseller, *On Tyranny.* The author of *Bloodlands: Europe Between Hitler and Stalin* and *Black Earth: The Holocaust as History and Warning,* Snyder writes that "Americans today are no wiser than the Europeans who saw democracy yield to fascism, Nazism, or communism in the twentieth century. Our one advantage is that we might learn from their experience."

He reminds us that the history of many modern democracies is "one of decline and fall" in circumstances "that in some important respects resemble our own." For instance, "both fascism and communism were responses to globalization: to the real and perceived inequalities it created, and the apparent helplessness of the democracies in addressing them." At the same time, elections alone guarantee nothing: some rulers destroy—or alter—the very institutions that brought them to power, turning those institutions into "a simulacrum of what they once were, so that they gird the new order rather than resisting it."

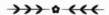

Steven Levitsky and Daniel Ziblatt, professors of government at Harvard University, make a similar observation in their 2018 book, *How Democracies Die.* They point out that elected leaders have subverted democratic institutions in Venezuela, Hungary, Poland, Russia, and Turkey. Many people, the authors add, continue to believe they are living in a democracy until it is too late, because "there is no single moment—no coup, declaration of martial law, or suspension of the constitution—in which the regime obviously 'crosses the line' into dictatorship."

Levitsky and Ziblatt note that in many cases (including that of Hitler), ruling elites legitimize the autocrat-in-the-making or provide entrée into mainstream politics out of self-interest, fear, or the mistaken belief that they can contain the demagogic outsider.

Signs that a new ruler is intent on subverting democracy, they write, include disrespect for a country's constitution; contempt for rivals, characterizing them not as legitimate opponents but as enemies of the people; threats against the press; and the undermining of civil liberties.

Autocrats do not usually shatter democratic institutions in one fell swoop, Levitsky and Ziblatt write. Rather, they tend to take a series of steps that initially go unnoticed by much of the public. Those steps include capturing the referees (putting loyalists in place at agencies and courts that have the power to arbitrate, implement, or challenge policies and laws); sidelining or defaming high-profile opponents and media outlets; changing the rules of the game (via techniques like gerrymandering and voter suppression) to lock in the ruler's (or party's) advantages for years; and degrading norms of tolerance and fairness that protect pluralistic dialogue and reasoned debate.

Ziblatt and Levitsky underscore the crucial role that crises—wars, terrorist attacks, natural disasters—can play in "the concentration and, very often, abuse of power." Citizens, they observe, are "more likely to tolerate—and even support—authoritarian measures during security crises, especially when they fear for their own safety," and authoritarians are poised to exploit such crises: the best-known case is Hitler's use of the Reichstag fire (which the Nazis might well have staged themselves) in early 1933 to justify emergency measures abolishing constitutional protections.

Vladimir Putin similarly exploited a series of bombings in Russian cities in 1999 (alleged by some to have been carried out by the Russian security service, the FSB) to start a second war in Chechnya, which boosted his approval ratings and fueled his ascent to the presidency the following year.

In his 2018 book, *The Road to Unfreedom,* Timothy Snyder astutely noted that this became a kind of go-to strategy for Putin to stay in power. Instead of grappling with Russia's real social and economic problems, he focused attention on exaggerated or fictional enemies who were said to be victimizing Russia; at the same time, he depicted himself as the country's virile "redeemer" while using blatant lies to sow cynicism and confusion.

In 2015, the Kremlin stepped up its disinformation efforts abroad, using Russian propaganda outlets (like Sputnik and RT) and social media platforms to spread fake news, while making alliances with right-wing groups to undermine democratic governments and institutions in Europe and the United States.

The election of Donald Trump was a big win for Vladimir Putin. Whereas influence in the 1990s and early years of the twenty-first century was flowing from west to east (with the spread of democratic economic and political models, and the enlargement of NATO and the European Union), Snyder writes, that flow began to reverse course in the following decade. Today, Snyder warns, concepts all too familiar to Russians—like "fake news," seemingly intractable social and economic inequalities, and declining faith in government—are, alarmingly, taking root in the West.

THE SIXTH EXTINCTION
An Unnatural History

(2014)

Elizabeth Kolbert

Five times in the history of the planet, something catastrophic happened that caused biodiversity to plummet, almost wiping out life. The fifth and most famous mass extinction occurred at the end of the Cretaceous period, when a giant asteroid struck the earth, killing off the non-avian dinosaurs, some three-quarters of all bird families, four-fifths of all lizards and snakes, and two-thirds of all mammals.

A sixth mass extinction is looming now, the *New Yorker* writer Elizabeth Kolbert writes in her clear-eyed and deeply alarming book, and this time the cause of this great dying off is not something from outer space. Rather, as Walt Kelly's Pogo observed many decades ago, "We have met the enemy, and they is us."

Human beings have introduced invasive species to places where they have destroyed the ecological balance. We've dammed rivers and chopped up the landscape, destroying natural habitats and impeding migration. And we've hunted animals and birds—from the passenger pigeon to the great auk to the Tasmanian tiger—into extinction. Most devastating of all, of course, is what we've done to the atmosphere. The cavalier burning of fossil fuels and the mowing down of the planet's great forests have raised the concentration of carbon dioxide in the air to the highest levels in 800,000 years—changes that have led to the rapid warming of the planet. These changes, in turn, have led to

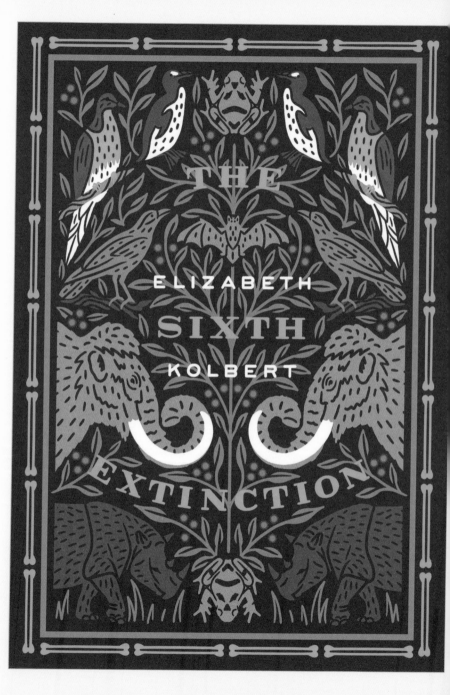

THE

ELIZABETH

SIXTH

KOLBERT

EXTINCTION

increasingly intense hurricanes, floods, droughts, wildfires, and acidic oceans—all of which is wreaking havoc on ecosystems. Rising sea levels threaten coastal cities, while rising temperatures are allowing viruses, bacteria, and disease-carrying insects to expand their range beyond the tropics.

"Warming today is taking place at least ten times faster than it did at the end of the last glaciation," Kolbert observes, and the fallout of human-driven change is devastating. "It is estimated," she writes, "that one-third of all reef-building corals, a third of all freshwater mollusks, a third of sharks and rays, a quarter of all mammals, a fifth of all reptiles, and a sixth of all birds are headed toward oblivion.

Kolbert writes with urgency and authority, situating recent headlines about climate change in historical perspective and using her skills as a reporter (much as she did in her 2006 book, *Field Notes from a Catastrophe*) to take us to the front lines, where researchers are studying how a variety of life-forms are struggling to adapt to accelerating shifts in their habitats. She visits an amphibian conservation center in Panama, where a mysterious fungus has been killing off rare frogs, and an Australian research station near the Great Barrier Reef, where scientists are monitoring the effects of ocean acidification on coral. Kolbert also gives us charming portraits of two endangered creatures—Kinohi, a solitary Hawaiian crow, and Suci, a Sumatran rhino, who are being encouraged, without a lot of success, to reproduce in captivity and who may be among the last of their kinds on the planet.

These are only two of the many animal species now threatened. In fact, by disrupting the systems that sustain life on the planet, Kolbert writes, "we're putting our own survival in danger." Or, as the Stanford ecologist Paul Ehrlich puts it, "in pushing other species to extinction, humanity is busy sawing off the limb on which it perches."

THE NAMESAKE

(2003)

Jhumpa Lahiri

The people in many of Jhumpa Lahiri's beautifully observed stories and novels are immigrants or the children of immigrants, trying to navigate a path in America while holding on to memories of their families back home in India. In one story, a couple who live near a small New England college used to begin each semester by perusing the university directory, "circling surnames familiar to their part of the world" in search of new friends. In another story, a girl tries to help give her younger brother a real American childhood, scouring yard sales for the right toy ("the Fisher Price barn, Tonka trucks, the Speak and Say that made animal sounds"), and tells her parents to set up lawn sprinklers in the summer so her brother can run through them the way other children do.

In her affecting debut novel, *The Namesake*—a Chekhovian story about loss and missed connections, exile and belonging—Lahiri drew an indelible portrait of members of the Ganguli family and their very different attitudes toward America. While Ashoke Ganguli had eagerly come to Boston to pursue a doctorate in engineering, his bride, Ashima—whom he married in an arranged ceremony—is frightened by the prospect of raising children "in a country where she is related to no one, where she knows so little." Their two children, eager to fit in with their friends, will find themselves constantly commuting between American and Bengali culture, between their parents' expectations and their own dreams and ambitions.

Lahiri has a remarkable eye for details—tiny, telling details that reveal the texture of daily life, and equally precise emotional details that disclose her characters' states of mind. Of a new house that the Gangulis move to in the Boston suburbs, Lahiri writes, "Their garage, like every other, contains shovels and pruning shears and a sled. They purchase a barbecue for tandoori on the porch in summer. Each step, each acquisition, no matter how small, involves deliberation, consultation with Bengali friends. Was there a difference between a plastic rake and a metal one? Which was preferable, a live Christmas tree or an artificial one? They learn to roast turkeys, albeit rubbed with garlic and cumin and cayenne, at Thanksgiving, to nail a wreath to their door in December, to wrap woolen scarves around snowmen, to color boiled eggs violet and pink at Easter and hide them around the house."

Such descriptions feel pitch perfect to me. I grew up in another New England suburb, and my father and my mother's parents were immigrants from Japan. Like Gary Shteyngart in *Little Failure*, Lahiri captures the carefulness, the sense of caution, that attended so many of my parents' decisions, whether it was buying a new toaster ("what does *Consumer Reports* say?") or planning a short trip (as though it would be impossible in another city or state to buy toothpaste or new socks). Anxious and conscientious, they worried about overdue library books and lapsed car registrations, saved cookie tins and marmalade jars (because "you never know when you might need one").

Lahiri writes that the Gangulis' house on Pemberton Road looks like all the other houses on the street, and that their children take bologna and roast beef sandwiches to school just like all their friends. And yet the family never feels quite at home in this pleasant suburb. News of their relatives in India comes through the mail or noisily by phone in the middle of the night.

The Gangulis' son Gogol initially tries to distance himself from his Indian roots: he does not hang out with other Indian American students, does not think of India as home, as his parents and their friends do, but as "India," like his American friends. Yet at the same time he often feels a sense of detachment, a slight sense of apartness.

Only after Ashoke's sudden death from a heart attack will Gogol fully appreciate what his father sacrificed to come to America so that his children would have the sorts of opportunities they wouldn't have had back home. And only when she plans to return to India, in the wake of her husband's death, will Ashima realize how much she'd come to love her adopted country: "For thirty-three years she missed her life in India. Now she will miss her job at the library, the women with whom she's worked. She will miss throwing parties. She will miss living with her daughter, the surprising companionship they have formed, going into Cambridge together to see old movies at the Brattle, teaching her to cook the food Sonia had complained of eating as a child. . . . She will miss the country in which she had grown to know and love her husband. Though his ashes have been scattered into the Ganges, it is here, in this house and in this town, that he will continue to dwell in her mind."

BOOKS BY JARON LANIER

YOU ARE NOT A GADGET: A Manifesto (2010)

DAWN OF THE NEW EVERYTHING:
Encounters with Reality and Virtual Reality (2017)

J aron Lanier is one of those rare polymaths who is equally fluent in the realms of science and art. He was a pioneer in the development of virtual reality, a member of Silicon Valley's founding generation that built the internet, a gifted musician and composer, and the author of several influential books addressing the cultural, social, and political consequences of today's social media and digital technology.

In the 1980s, Lanier was a member of what he calls "a merry band of idealists" who hoped that the digital revolution would release a tsunami of creativity and innovation and foster more felicitous communication among people. He believed that virtual reality—as a "medium that can put you in someone else's shoes"—could create "a path to increased empathy."

By the mid-1990s, Lanier was already writing about some of the pitfalls he saw developing on "the infobahn." In a 1995 essay titled "Agents of Alienation," he essentially predicted the problems we face today with Big Tech giants like Facebook and Google trying to maximize user engagement (and hence, ad revenues) by using algorithms, based on our past choices and preexisting beliefs, to customize what we see in our news feeds and search results—a development that has had the effect of isolating people in filter bubbles and partisan silos and contributed to an increasingly tribalized world.

If "intelligent agents" control what we, the info consumers, see, Lanier wrote two and a half decades ago, "then advertising will transform into the art of controlling agents," and a "new information bottleneck" will narrow "the otherwise delightfully anarchic infobahn, which was supposed to replace the broadcast model with something more inclusive." An agent's (or algorithm's) model of "what you are interested in will be a cartoon model," he adds, "and you will see a cartoon version of the world through the agent's eyes. It is therefore a self-reinforcing model. This will recreate the lowest-common-denominator approach to content that plagues TV."

In such provocative books as *You Are Not a Gadget* and *Dawn of the New Everything,* Lanier amplified such arguments while making an eloquent case for "a new digital humanism" that would prize individuality over "the hive mind." The economics of free internet content, he reminded us, has created a reliance on advertising as a source of revenue while making it difficult for creators of content— that is, writers, artists, musicians, journalists—to earn a living.

In *You Are Not a Gadget,* Lanier observed that software engineers' design decisions had the power to fundamentally shape users' behavior. Much the way that decisions about the dimensions of railroad tracks determined the size and velocity of trains for decades to come, he argued, choices made about software design in the formative years of the internet created "defining, unchangeable rules" for generations to come through the process known as lock-in.

Decisions that promoted online anonymity, for instance, have had all manner of unforeseen consequences, enabling trolling, digital scams, and online mob attacks, as well as the flood of propaganda, disinformation, and fake news that played such an alarming role in the 2016 presidential election and Brexit referendum.

Lanier's books are informed by his insider's knowledge of Silicon Valley technology and his concerns about the effects that technology is having on our thinking and our everyday lives—from the shallow, status-conscious interactions encouraged by social media, to the recycled culture of nostalgia and mash-ups promoted by a web in which originality often seems in short supply.

In *Dawn of the New Everything*, Lanier also recounts the strange, winding road that first brought him to Palo Alto—from his childhood on the Texas-Mexico border, where his bohemian parents nurtured his love of both art and technology, to his work on an early video game named *Moondust*, to his experiments in virtual reality with the coder Tom Zimmerman. In fact, Lanier's own life story makes for fascinating reading—a moving and inspiring account of a modern-day Renaissance man.

A WRINKLE IN TIME

(1962)

Madeleine L'Engle

A Wrinkle in Time was one of the first books I felt I had discovered on my own—even though a librarian at the local public library had gently steered me toward it. I identified with its heroine, Meg Murry—not only because she was an awkward kid who felt like an outsider, but because she had a dad who was a scientist (and my father was a mathematician, engaged in incomprehensible work that seemed to touch, in some vague way, on the secrets of the universe). Meg was an unlikely heroine for a science-fiction book in the 1960s—a nerdy, bespectacled kid, whose curiosity about the world was matched only by her impatience with the frustrations of school and daily life.

Meg, along with her genius five-year-old brother, Charles Wallace, and her schoolmate Calvin O'Keefe, travels through time and space with an assist from three supernatural creatures who go by the names of Mrs. Whatsit, Mrs. Who, and Mrs. Which. Their mission: to rescue her father, who has been taken captive by a giant disembodied brain called IT, on a faraway planet named Camazotz, where people live regimented, obedient lives. If the threat posed by IT—intelligence divorced from emotion and disdainful of individuality—now feels like an uncanny warning about the dangers of worshipping technology and AI, Camazotz represents a kind of dystopian world of conformity, embodied in the 1950s by the bogeymen of communism, on the one hand, and capitalistic groupthink, on the other.

Mrs. Whatsit reminds the children that the people on Camazotz lead entirely planned lives, devoid of surprise and creativity and choice. She urges them to recognize the value of freedom and compares life to a sonnet: "You're given the form, but you have to write the sonnet yourself. What you say is completely up to you." Charles tries to explain the mysteries of traveling through space and time via a shortcut called the tesseract, observing that sometimes "a straight line is not the shortest distance between two points."

Like the *Harry Potter* books, *A Wrinkle in Time* featured courageous children who help lead the battle against the forces of evil in the world, and a protagonist who recognizes the power of love to save a family member's life. In many ways, Meg Murry was a kind of older cousin to Hermione and to the spirited and resourceful heroines like Katniss in the *Hunger Games* books and Tris in the *Divergent* novels, who decades later would captivate new generations of readers.

 *Meg was an unlikely heroine for a science-fiction book in the 1960s—a nerdy, bespectacled kid, whose curiosity about the world was matched only by her impatience with the frustrations of school and daily life.*

ABRAHAM LINCOLN BOOKS

THE SPEECHES AND WRITINGS OF ABRAHAM LINCOLN (2018)
Edited by Don E. Fehrenbacher for Library of America

LINCOLN AT GETTYSBURG: The Words That Remade America
(1992) Garry Wills

LINCOLN: The Biography of a Writer (2008)
Fred Kaplan

LINCOLN'S SWORD: The Presidency and the Power of Words (2006)
Douglas L. Wilson

>>> ✿ <<<

With 272 words in a three-minute speech delivered on the bloodied fields of Gettysburg on a November day in 1863, Abraham Lincoln not only changed how America would think about the Civil War—he framed how future generations would understand the founding principles of the United States.

As Garry Wills brilliantly explained in his 1992 book, *Lincoln at Gettysburg,* the sixteenth president was undertaking, with his remarks, "a new founding of the nation" that harked back to the Declaration of Independence with its promise of equality and liberty for all. Lincoln, in his wisdom, understood that America was an ongoing project and that a more perfect union would require the living to dedicate themselves to "the unfinished work" that those who fought on the battlefield at Gettysburg had advanced—arduous, frustrating, and courageous work that continues to this day.

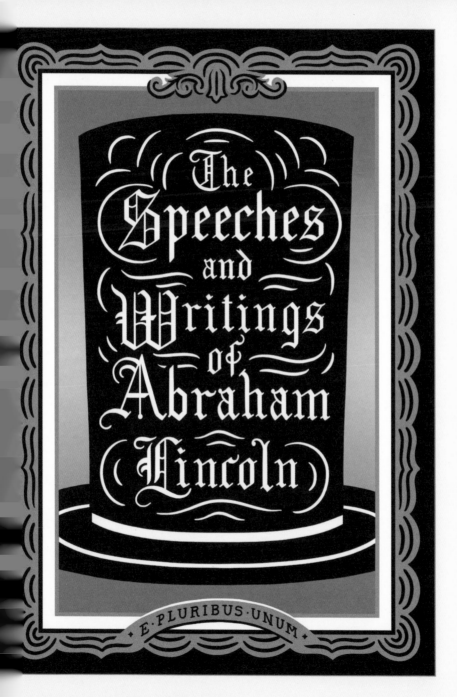

It was a theme Lincoln would return to in his second inaugural address—a speech that sought to heal the nation's wounds and divisions, and also called upon Americans to "strive on to finish the work we are in."

Lincoln's ability to use his words to enlist the nation in achieving its ideals was rooted in his dual gifts: his poetic love of language and storytelling, nurtured by the voracious reading he'd done since he was a boy; and his skill, as a lawyer, in the art of persuasion. Reading through a volume of his collected speeches and letters, we see how Lincoln found a voice of his own over the years that expressed the full range of his personality—from the pensive and elegiac, to the humorous and playful, to the urgent and instructive. It was a voice supple enough to accommodate everything from folksy storytelling to inspiring visions of a world responsive to "the better angels of our nature."

Many of Lincoln's biographers have commented upon his literary gifts. A couple books stand out in particular. In *Lincoln: The Biography of a Writer,* Fred Kaplan examines just how pivotal a role Shakespeare and the Bible played in shaping the young Lincoln's sensibility. Shakespeare remained a primary touchstone throughout Lincoln's life, Kaplan observes, molding his almost existential view of mankind's plight in a random, unpredictable world, while Aesop's fables fueled his own use of storytelling as a means of illustration and moral argument.

In *Lincoln's Sword: The Presidency and the Power of Words,* Douglas L. Wilson suggests that writing, for the president, was a form of refuge, "a place of intellectual retreat from the chaos and confusion of office where he could sort through conflicting options, and order his thoughts with words." According to Wilson, Lincoln "habitually made notes on scraps of paper of ideas that occurred to him." The president's former law partner William Herndon recalled that in preparing his "House Divided" speech, he stored those bits of paper in his hat; later, he arranged them in the right order and wrote out the speech.

In preparing a speech, Lincoln would frequently read the text aloud to friends or aides—to gauge how the words played to an audience—and he would also make numerous revisions to a text, as manuscripts in the Library of Congress attest. The reading aloud and the constant revisions, Garry Wills argues, helped hone Lincoln's language, making it simpler, more precise, more economical—in contrast to writing (and speech making) of the day, which inclined toward artifice and grandiosity. Lincoln's remarks at Gettysburg, Wills adds, "anticipated the shift to vernacular rhythms that Mark Twain would complete twenty years later. Hemingway claimed that all modern American novels are the offspring of *Huckleberry Finn*. It is no greater exaggeration to say that all modern political prose descends from the Gettysburg Address."

ARCTIC DREAMS
Imagination and Desire in a Northern Landscape

(1986)

Barry Lopez

B ritish and American novels—from classics like Mary
Shelley's *Frankenstein* to more recent works like Andrea
Barrett's *Voyage of the Narwhal* (1998) and Ian McGuire's
North Water (2016)—have often depicted the Arctic as an icy
landscape of extremes that becomes a kind of primordial testing
ground, a place where human ambition and greed play out in
violence or death.

Today, with accelerating climate change, the Arctic itself has
become a victim of human hubris. Recent studies indicate that
the region is warming at twice the rate of the rest of the planet and
suffers from an unforgiving feedback loop: because ice and snow
reflect sunlight while open water absorbs it, melting causes further
warming, which causes further melting, and so on. These rising
temperatures, in turn, bring changes to the sea ice, snow cover, and
permafrost below, and they threaten the way of life of people and
animals who live there. They also lead to a cascade of consequences
across the globe including rising sea levels, increased ocean acidity,
and more extreme weather.

Given these alarming developments, Barry Lopez's 1986 book,
Arctic Dreams, reads today as both a great classic of wilderness
writing and an elegiac tribute to a vanishing world. Drawing upon
the work of geologists, explorers, anthropologists, archaeologists,

and biologists, in addition to assorted myths and bits of Eskimo lore, Lopez gives us an impressionistic picture of the North, communicating an elemental sense of the wonder and awe he experienced during a four-to-five-year-long journey through these lands.

For Lopez, the Arctic is a place that exists not only in the mathematics of geography but also in the terra incognita of our imaginations. It's a land where "airplanes track icebergs the size of Cleveland and polar bears fly down out of the stars," a land rich in imagery and metaphor, where the moon can shine for a week and the sun may disappear for days.

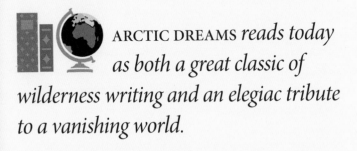 ARCTIC DREAMS *reads today as both a great classic of wilderness writing and an elegiac tribute to a vanishing world.*

His narrative loops back and forth between the philosophical and the scientific, the metaphorical and the specific. He describes what it feels like to be a nineteenth-century whaler coming upon the "loveliness and grandeur" of this uncharted, unclaimed land for the first time. And he describes the heavenly, hallucinatory quality of light found in the high, thin air of the Arctic and how delicately and suddenly it can shift.

What initially seems like an austere, utterly monotonous landscape, Lopez shows us, is actually a remarkably complex ecosystem. In the migratory routes of birds and animals, as in the travel routes of early human settlers, there are intricate, overlapping patterns dictated by the geography of the land, seasonal shifts in sunlight, and the biological rhythms of survival.

Lopez's writing about animal life in the Arctic possesses the closely observed detail of a scientific paper and the narrative verve of a novel. We learn that polar bears are so well insulated that they have trouble getting rid of excess heat (which they are said to deal with by eating snow), that they build dens using the same principles of architecture employed by Eskimos in building igloos, and that ancient legends say they cover their dark noses with a paw or a piece of snow so as to sneak up on seals unobserved.

The different attitudes toward the land evinced by Eskimos and Western visitors to the Arctic lie at the heart of this book. "The great task of life for the traditional Eskimo is still to achieve congruence with a reality that is already given," Lopez writes— to have a "conversation with the land," which stands in sharp contrast to the Western belief that "the conditions of the earth can be changed to ensure human happiness, to provide jobs and to create material wealth and ease."

"Eskimos," he goes on, "who sometimes see themselves as still not quite separate from the animal world, regard us as a kind of people whose separation may have become too complete. They call us, with a mixture of incredulity and apprehension, 'the people who change nature.'"

It's an observation that has taken on an ominous new meaning today as human-induced warming has become an existential threat to the Arctic—and the entire planet.

BLOOD MERIDIAN, OR, THE EVENING REDNESS IN THE WEST

(1985)

Cormac McCarthy

*B*lood Meridian will give you nightmares.

The story is almost unrelievedly violent and blood soaked and represents the grimmest, most primal distillation of the author's Hobbesian view of the world. With *Blood Meridian,* Cormac McCarthy also created a potent retelling of America's myth of the western frontier, leaving us with an ineradicable understanding of the costs in lives and suffering caused by the wars of extermination waged against Native Americans, and the policies of expulsion that enabled the theft of their ancestral lands. In fact, the novel exposes the dark imperialism at the heart of the doctrine of Manifest Destiny, which would be used to justify both America's westward territorial expansion and later adventures abroad.

Based in part on historical events in the Southwest circa 1849–1850, *Blood Meridian* recounts the story of a notorious group of scalp hunters who collect bounties for the Apaches and Mexicans they massacre. They are driven by cruelty, racism, greed, and bloodlust.

Among these killers is a teenage boy whom McCarthy refers to, generically, as "the kid," who seems to hold on to a "corner of clemency for the heathen" in the midst of all this horror. And presiding over the horror is Judge Holden, a huge, pale monster of a man, given to making nihilistic speeches and dancing naked—an incarnation of Satan who claims he never sleeps and will never die. The only man who has truly lived, the judge says, is the "man who has offered up himself entire to the blood of war, who has been to the floor of the pit and seen horror in the round and learned at last that it speaks to his inmost heart."

The judge must rank up there as one of the most frightening villains in literature—as towering a figure of evil as Milton's Lucifer, and reminiscent in demeanor and symbolic import of Colonel Kurtz, played by Marlon Brando in the 1979 movie *Apocalypse Now* (a role based on the corrupt ivory trader turned madman in Conrad's *Heart of Darkness*).

In one sequence, the judge rescues an Apache boy from a raid, allows him refuge for a couple days, and then calmly scalps him. When another character says "might does not make right," the judge replies, "Moral law is an invention of mankind for the disenfranchisement of the powerful in favor of the weak."

McCarthy's writing in *Blood Meridian* is, at once, operatic and Faulknerian. He chronicles the death of countless people in terms that are part Grand Guignol theater, part Jacobean drama, part *Game of Thrones*. Other scenes have a haunting, cinematic quality. McCarthy describes a group of Indians emerging from the dust, mounted on horses, and wearing costumes "out of a fevered dream" with animal skins mixed with "pieces of uniform still tracked with the blood of prior owners," one wearing a stovepipe hat, another wielding an umbrella. And he conjures the Southwest landscape as a hellscape that is hard and barren and stony. It's a dismal landscape, delineated in minute detail, that is a mirror of McCarthy's pitiless vision of mankind engaged in an eternal battle with evil, and an American history rooted in racism and heartsickening violence.

ATONEMENT

(2001)

Ian McEwan

Ian McEwan's remarkable novel *Atonement* is a love story, a war story, and a story about the destructive powers of the imagination. It is also a remarkable tour de force—one of those novels that gains in resonance and nuance with every reading.

The novel pivots around a terrible lie told by a thirteen-year-old girl named Briony Tallis—one motivated by jealousy, spite, an appetite for melodrama, and a willful naïveté about the workings of the grown-up world. Briony's false accusations will send her older sister's lover Robbie away to jail and shatter the family's staid, upper-middle-class existence. They will expose psychological fault lines running through family members' lives while making us aware of the festering class tensions that existed in England of the 1930s and the momentous social changes that World War II would usher in.

At the same time, the novel—which has supposedly been written by one of its characters—emerges as a sophisticated rumination on the hazards of fantasy and the chasm between reality and art. Its myriad allusions (to such disparate novels as *Clarissa, Northanger Abbey, Lady Chatterley's Lover, Howards End,* and *Mrs. Dalloway*) situate the story within a rich literary matrix, even as they italicize the artifice involved in creating a work of fiction—the tidying up of real-life loose ends made in the service of manufacturing a satisfying tale.

ATONEMENT

IAN McEWAN

In earlier novels like *The Innocent* and *Amsterdam,* McEwan used his gifts as a ventriloquist to put across the point of view of decidedly unsavory characters, and in *Atonement* he manages to make the state of mind that leads Briony to make her false accusations against Robbie plausible, if not sympathetic. He shows how her petulance and self-dramatizing imagination lead her to ignore the truth, how her ignorance about the grown-up world results in loss and devastation that she will spend her adult life trying to rationalize and atone for.

The part of the novel tracing the fallout of Briony's lies on the Tallis family includes a devastating account of the 1940 Allied retreat from Dunkirk, as seen from the point of view of Robbie, who won an early release from prison in return for joining the infantry. It's a sequence that could stand alone as a bravura set piece capturing the banality and horror of war with astonishing verisimilitude.

Atonement takes the glittering narrative pyrotechnics McEwan perfected in earlier works and employs them in the service of a larger, tragic vision. It also takes his perennial themes (dealing with the hazards of innocence, the hold of time past over time present, and the intrusion of evil into ordinary lives) and orchestrates them into a symphonic work that is every bit as affecting as it is compelling.

MOBY-DICK

(1851)

Herman Melville

*M*oby-Dick had a reputation in high school and college as a tedious, absurdly overstuffed novel (about whales, of all things!), and many students winced when they saw it on a syllabus, thinking they were in for a long, boring slog of a read. And yet, once we started reading it, many of us discovered that it was actually an amazingly strange and magical book—completely innovative in its trippy, encyclopedic approach to the world and written in mesmerizing language that managed to be biblical and Shakespearean and oddly slangy, all at the same time.

I still have my copy of the book—a Norton Critical Edition paperback, purchased, used, for one dollar at Whitlock's Book Barn, this great vintage bookshop, housed in two old barns in Bethany, Connecticut. My copy is filled with underlinings and notes in ballpoint pen from its previous owner, and my own annotations made with a Flair pen—lots of exclamation points and instances of "yes!" in my polite, schoolgirl's script.

I fell in love with the book, in part, because I was lucky enough to have a wonderful teacher, Richard B. Sewall, who made *Moby-Dick,* and works by Shakespeare, Milton, and Dostoyevsky, feel palpably real and urgent—great works of literature that were not dusty old classics but daring, inventive books that addressed the eternal questions humankind grapples with: essential questions about our relationship with God and Nature and Fate, and the soaring possibilities and stark limitations of human understanding.

Moby-Dick was, at once, an exploration of the dichotomies in the world between good and evil, order and chaos, land and water; a challenge to the sunny optimism of the transcendentalists; an allegory about class and race in America as the country lurched toward civil war; and an encyclopedic anatomy of whales and whaling, meant as a kind of representation of humanity's flailing and ineffectual efforts to catalog and make sense of the world.

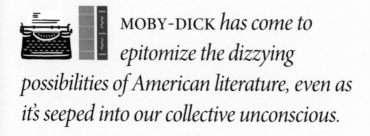 MOBY-DICK *has come to epitomize the dizzying possibilities of American literature, even as it's seeped into our collective unconscious.*

Melville, who was only thirty years old when he began the book, wrote it—shockingly—in less than two years. And he tackled his "mighty book" with every device in his writer's toolkit: poetic prose that gyrated between the incantatory and the vernacular, the oracular and the comic; an insane mash-up of literary devices (including quotations, philosophical asides, scientific taxonomies, soliloquies, dramatic dialogues, and a fusillade of similes and metaphors and word-drunk digressions); and mind-bogglingly detailed accounts of every aspect of whaling and whales imaginable (from descriptions of the dangers of harpooning to the arduous process of extracting oil from the blubber, to a disquisition on the varieties of whales and their anatomy).

Even as the novel remained grounded in the visceral details of seamanship that Melville, as a young sailor, had observed firsthand, it addressed the most abstract metaphysical questions. Generations of students would write papers about the novel's allegorical meanings. The whale could be seen as everything from "the utmost monster of the seas" symbolizing the untamable powers of Nature, to nothing but a large white mammal upon whom men could project their own dark imaginings. As for Ahab, he could be described as a Shakespearean villain in thrall to a mad obsession or as a symbol of American hubris, imposing his folly on the entire crew of the *Pequod*, rushing headlong into catastrophe (think: the Civil War, Vietnam, Iraq, climate change).

For all these reasons, *Moby-Dick* has come to epitomize the dizzying possibilities of American literature, even as it's seeped into our collective unconscious. The novel has inspired work by artists like Laurie Anderson, Frank Stella, Led Zeppelin, and Bernard Herrmann, and directly or indirectly influenced such disparate writers as David Foster Wallace, Dave Eggers, Norman Mailer, and Roberto Bolaño. There's *Jaws*, of course, but many others too. The beginning and end of *The Great Gatsby*—not to mention, Fitzgerald's use of an Ishmael-like narrator—remind me of *Moby-Dick*. The *Star Trek* movie *The Wrath of Khan* invokes Ahab's story, and there are allusions or references to *Moby-Dick* in Cormac McCarthy's *Blood Meridian* and Hart Crane's poems. Once you read or reread *Moby-Dick,* you start seeing the great white whale and his relentless pursuer everywhere.

A GATE AT THE STAIRS

(2009)

Lorrie Moore

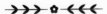

The title of Lorrie Moore's heartbreaking novel *A Gate at the Stairs* comes from a song that her heroine, a college student and sometime musician, writes:

> *Did you take off for Heaven*
> *and leave me behind?*
> *Darlin', I'd join you*
> *if you didn't mind.*
> *I'd climb up that staircase*
> *past lions and bears,*
> *but it's locked*
> *at the foot of the stairs.*

Never mind the corny lyrics. Moore's novel gives us an enduring portrait of a young woman coming of age in the Midwest in the year after 9/11 and her initiation into the adult world of loss and grief.

Like Alice McDermott's *Charming Billy* and *At Weddings and Wakes,* this novel explores, with exacting emotional precision, the promises and insufficiencies of love, and the loneliness that haunts even the most doting of families. While very funny at times, it is concerned at heart with the consequences of carelessness—of failing to pay attention to, or fight for, those one loves, and the random, out-of-the-blue events, not unlike 9/11, that can abruptly torpedo or transform a life.

The narrator of *Stairs* is one Tassie Keltjin, who is looking back on her twentieth year. Having grown up on a small midwestern farm, Tassie has never taken a taxi or an airplane, never eaten Chinese food, never seen a man wear jeans with a shirt and tie. Though her brother, Robert, who is desultorily thinking of joining the military, looks up to her as a focused, surefooted college girl, she thinks of herself as lost, as lacking the ambitions of friends ("marriage, children, law school") and lacking an internal gyroscope that might lend ballast to her plans.

Enrollment at a liberal-minded midwestern college (where political correctness is de rigueur and students can take courses in things like wine tasting, war-movie soundtracks, and Pilates) has made Tassie feel as if she'd been led out of a cave into "a brilliant city life."

It's Tassie's part-time job as a nanny for a middle-aged couple, however, that will irrevocably alter her apprehension of the world. Sarah Brink runs a fancy restaurant called Le Petit Moulin, and her husband, Edward, is a cancer researcher. They have moved to Troy from the East and have just submitted adoption papers for a two-year-old, mixed-race girl they have named Mary-Emma. Tassie bonds with the little girl almost immediately, and her days soon settle into a pleasant rhythm of classes, afternoon walks, and play sessions with Mary-Emma. Evenings she often spends with a handsome classmate named Reynaldo who says he is from Brazil.

Neither Reynaldo nor Sarah and Edward turn out to be who they say they are. This is not just a matter of their duplicity or Tassie's naïveté; it's also about the costs of impulsivity and romantic infatuation and the consequences of self-absorption.

After suffering three terrible losses, Tassie learns how bereavement can render one "passive, translucent, and demolished"; how the accumulation of bad luck can strafe a person "to the thinness of a nightgown"; how love—for a man, a child, a sibling—can make one more vulnerable to (not safer from) the calamities of life. Writing with affection and an instinctive grasp of the improbabilities of life, Moore gives us bright, digital snapshots of the Midwest, where nearly every small town has a Dairy Queen, where customers wait in lines, even in winter, and where the "whimsy and fuss" of homeowners' Christmas decorations—"penguins, palm trees, geese, and candy canes all lit up as if they were long-lost friends at a gathering"— provide a seasonal diversion for neighbors.

Moore makes us see Tassie's family farm, where her mother has set up mirrors behind the flower beds to multiply the foxgloves and nightshades and phlox and where her father used to have her don a hawk costume and run in front of his thresher to scare wildlife from its hiding places. ("Nobody wanted sliced mice in their salads," she drily observes, "at least not this decade.")

Most memorably, Moore gives us stark, melancholy glimpses into her characters' hearts, mapping their fears and disappointments, their hidden yearnings, and their efforts to hold on to their dreams in the face of unfurling misfortune and the precariousness of daily life.

BOOKS BY TONI MORRISON

SONG OF SOLOMON (1977)

BELOVED (1987)

In novels spanning several hundred years of history, Toni Morrison used her historical imagination and her remarkable gifts of language to chronicle the horrors of slavery and Jim Crow and their continuing fallout on the everyday lives of black Americans.

Violent, heart-wrenching events occur in her fiction: a runaway slave named Sethe cuts the throat of her baby daughter with a handsaw to spare her the fate she suffered herself as a slave (*Beloved*); a woman pours kerosene on her drug-addicted son and sets him on fire (*Sula*). Such horrifying events are acts of desperation that can be comprehended only in context with the earlier tragedies these characters or their families have suffered. In fact, if there is one insistent theme in Morrison's novels, it's the ways in which the past inexorably shapes the present, trampling innocence, cutting off options of escape, and warping relationships between women and men, parents and children.

As in Faulkner's work, the past is never dead for Morrison's people; it's not even past. Faulkner was clearly an influence on Morrison's writing, and so were Ralph Ellison, Virginia Woolf, Gabriel García Márquez, and African American folklore. But Morrison forged from such disparate sources a voice that was all her own—fierce, poetic, and Proustian in its ability to fuse memory and experience.

Her 1987 masterpiece, *Beloved,* created a harrowing portrait of slavery that possesses all the resonance of a classical myth while remaining grounded in the awful particulars of American history. And her haunting 1977 novel, *Song of Solomon,* stands as a quintessential bildungsroman—the story of one man's coming of age and rebirth, recounted in a narrative that spans allegory, realism, and fable.

Strange, surreal events proliferate in Morrison's books: there are ghosts and voodoo dolls, men who think they can fly, bags of bones dangling from the ceiling. Such fantastical matters are taken for granted by Morrison's people. Given the cruelties of history they have witnessed—bodies hanging from trees, forty-six men chained together in the blazing Georgia sun—the bizarre and monstrous no longer surprise. It's the ordinary that too often seems out of reach.

An awareness of the impermanence of life haunts Morrison's people. Many of them are orphans: people who have experienced abandonment as children or as spurned romantic partners. In the words of one of her heroines, they feel themselves to be ice floes, "cut away from the riverbank," and they yearn to find something to belong to. At the same time, they are wary of caring too much. After all, loss and leaving are all too likely to result: parents die, children grow up, lovers move on, land is sold or stolen, people are killed or jailed. The luckier ones realize that the past must sometimes be left behind, that redemption is to be found not in obsessively remembering but in forgetting, if not forgiving. "Wanna fly," the best friend of the hero in *Song of Solomon* says, "you got to give up the shit that weighs you down."

Indeed transcendence always remains a possibility for the women and men in Morrison's novels—whether it's coming to appreciate "the music the world makes" or finding love, in the words of a character in *Beloved,* with someone who takes "the pieces I am" and gives them "back to me in all the right order."

BOOKS BY VLADIMIR NABOKOV

THE STORIES OF VLADIMIR NABOKOV (1995)
Edited by Dmitri Nabokov

SPEAK, MEMORY: An Autobiography Revisited (1951)

*T*he Stories of Vladimir Nabokov gives us a magical
retrospective of the master sorcerer Vladimir Nabokov's
career. His preoccupation with the interface between life
and art, his concern with the workings of memory and time, and
his delight in chess-like games—all combine in these pages to create
a kaleidoscopic array of stories: sharply edged allegorical fables;
quirky portraits of eccentric characters; sly, postmodernist puzzles.

Many of the early stories radiate a youthful beguilement with
the sensuousness of the world, a belief in "the profound beneficence
of all that surrounded me, the blissful bond between me and all of
creation." In later stories, Nabokov's rapturous embrace of life ("How
can death exist when they lead camels along a springtime street?")
gives way to more self-conscious, lapidary musings and dark
apprehensions of mortality. The thirty-three-year-old hero in one
story becomes so fearful of dying that he starts taking "extraordinary
measures to protect his life from the claims of fate": he stops going
out, stops shaving, spends more and more time in bed.

Nabokov's myriad gifts as a writer are on display throughout
this glittering volume of stories: his narrative ingenuity, his musical
command of language, his love of detail and precision (honed to

a fine edge by his two favorite hobbies, studying butterflies and playing chess); his ability to evoke a scene, a memory, a sensation or mood with pictorial immediacy and virtuosic sleight of hand. Gifts that explain his enduring influence over writers as disparate as John Updike, Thomas Pynchon, Martin Amis, Don DeLillo, and Zadie Smith. Even Justice Ruth Bader Ginsburg, who studied under Nabokov at Cornell University as an undergraduate, said he changed the way she read and the way she wrote: "He taught me the importance of choosing the right word and presenting it in the right word order."

Nabokov once compared novelists to God, arguing that "the real writer"—"the fellow who sends planets spinning and models a man asleep and eagerly tampers with the sleeper's rib"—is someone who takes the chaos of reality, recombines its atoms, and maps and names it. And in his own fiction, he could come across as a high-handed puppeteer, coldly dealing out death and disappointment to his unfortunate characters. This is the chilly, detached Nabokov who famously dispensed with the narrator's mother in *Lolita* with a two-word parenthesis: "(picnic, lightning)." He got rid of the pretty heroines in "A Russian Beauty" and "Spring in Fialta" in a few sentences, and in "The Return of Chorb" he deprived the poor hero of his new bride in a paragraph.

If such stories have won Nabokov a reputation for heartlessness, there is also a strain of heartfelt melancholy in these tales, rooted in his experience as an exile and émigré and his acute awareness of the evanescence of life. He grew up in a wealthy, aristocratic family in prerevolutionary Russia—a world beautifully conjured in his luminous, Proustian memoir, *Speak, Memory*—and would be twice displaced. In 1919, his family fled the Bolsheviks and eventually settled in Berlin, where his father was killed by a right-wing fanatic.

In 1940, after several desperate years of seeking an exit from Europe, Nabokov, his wife, Vera, and their son, Dmitri, found passage to America—a month before Paris fell to the Nazis.

Giving up his native language ("my untrammeled, rich, and infinitely docile Russian tongue") for a "second-rate brand of English," he once complained, was like "a champion figure skater switching to roller skates."

In America, Nabokov found jobs teaching at Wellesley and later Cornell University; during the summers, he and Vera would drive around the West in an Oldsmobile, logging more than 200,000 miles in search of butterflies in places like the Rocky Mountains and the Grand Canyon.

Nabokov came to love what he called this "lovely, trustful, dreamy, enormous country," but the sense of loss that comes with exile—the loss of home, the loss of a language—runs like an electrical current through *Speak, Memory* and many of these stories, surfacing in the missed connections and broken promises endured by his characters, as well as grief, divorce, and death.

In one poignant account (which appears in both *Speak, Memory* and this collection of stories), Nabokov memorializes his childhood governess with an odd mixture of poison and compassion. Near the end of the tale, he asks himself whether "during the years I knew her, I had not kept utterly missing something in her that was far more she than her chins or her ways or even her French." It was something, he later realized, that he "could appreciate only after the things and beings that I had most loved in the security of my childhood had been turned to ashes or shot through the heart."

READING LOLITA IN TEHRAN
A Memoir in Books

(2003)

Azar Nafisi

Azar Nafisi's 2003 book, *Reading Lolita in Tehran,* is an affecting memoir, a chilling account of life in Iran under the rule of the mullahs, and most powerfully, a biography of a book club that was transformative for Nafisi and her students—leaving them with an understanding of how fiction can offer a refuge from ideology, freedom from the daily grip of tyranny, and a subversive affirmation of the voice of the individual.

Before she left Iran in 1997 for the United States, Nafisi—who taught literature at several Iranian universities—held a reading group at her home in Tehran for some of her former students. Even on campus, she and many of her students had been assailed by the authorities for not wearing the veil, for not wearing it properly, for refusing to espouse a hard-line ideological stance, and for studying decadent Western texts. Members of her reading groups held a spectrum of political and religious views, and they were initially shy about sharing their opinions. But they slowly came to regard their weekly meetings as a kind of sanctuary, as a place where they could share confidences about everything from their dreams and ambitions, to their frustrations with the government, to their relationships with men—subjects they were able to broach by first discussing them in terms of the books they were reading.

Her students soon formed a special bond, Nafisi remembers, with the works of Nabokov, most notably *Invitation to a Beheading,* with its lonely, imaginative hero whose originality sets him apart in a society "where uniformity is not only the norm but also the law," and *Lolita,* which Nafisi reads as a disturbing story about "the confiscation of one individual's life by another." Her students' identification with this Russian émigré's works, she notes, went deeper than their identification with his themes, to a shared sense of the capriciousness of life. "His novels are shaped around invisible trapdoors, sudden gaps that constantly pull the carpet from under the reader's feet," she writes. "They are filled with mistrust of what we call everyday reality, an acute sense of that reality's fickleness and frailty."

 This, too, is why Nafisi regards the novel as a "democratic" form of art: through empathy and the imagination, it allows readers to understand the experience of others.

Nafisi's students find the work of F. Scott Fitzgerald and Henry James resonant too. They draw an analogy between Gatsby's thwarted efforts to repeat the past and the Iranian revolution, "which had come in the name of our collective past and had wrecked our lives in the name of a dream." And they regard Henry James's heroines Daisy Miller and Catherine Sloper as women who "defy the conventions of their time," who "refuse to be dictated to."

The absence of sympathy and compassion, Nafisi observes, is a quality shared by many of the villainous characters in novels she has taught over the years: assorted James personages (including the father and the suitor in *Washington Square*); "Nabokov's monster heroes: Humbert, Kinbote, Van and Ada Veen"; and the careless, narcissistic Buchanans in *The Great Gatsby*.

"The biggest sin is to be blind to others' problems and pains," Nafisi writes. "Not seeing them means denying their existence."

For that matter, she adds, the villain in modern fiction could well be described as "a creature without compassion, without empathy," who will violate another individual's rights and self-respect. It's a definition of evil she says most of her students in Iran shared "because it was so close to their own experience. Lack of empathy was to my mind the central sin of the regime, from which all the others flowed."

And this, too, is why Nafisi regards the novel as a "democratic" form of art: through empathy and the imagination, it allows readers to understand the experience of others. "A good novel is one that shows the complexity of individuals, and creates enough space for all these characters to have a voice," she writes. And "a great novel heightens your senses and sensitivity to the complexities of life and of individuals, and prevents you from the self-righteousness that sees morality in fixed formulas about good and evil."

A HOUSE FOR MR. BISWAS

(1961)

V. S. Naipaul

V. S. Naipaul's fiction and nonfiction grappled with themes that would fuel many of the twenty-first century's most critical and contentious debates: the relationship between the developing world and the West, the ongoing fallout of colonial oppression and postcolonial chaos, escalating tensions between tradition and modernity, and the sense of dislocation and cultural vertigo experienced by migrants and exiles in an increasingly globalized world.

Naipaul's fascination with these issues grew out of his own life, growing up in Trinidad, the grandson of an indentured laborer from India, and determined, from an early age, to escape his provincial upbringing and become a writer. He earned a scholarship to Oxford, became an eminent man of letters in London, and in 2001 won the Nobel Prize in Literature. The sense of being an outsider, however, never left him.

Some of Naipaul's later writings about what he called "half-made societies," places in Africa, the Caribbean, Latin America, and the Middle East, where "the West is packing its boxes, waiting for the helicopters," were warped by his contempt for his subjects—his bitter, misanthropic view of human nature, and the accusations of ignorance, superstition, and passivity he hurled at the developing world. Naipaul acknowledged the personal roots of this scorn and how it stemmed from defensiveness and his youthful fear of vulnerability and shame. In his 1961 novel, *A House for Mr. Biswas,* he wrote this of Anand, the title character's gifted literary son, who is clearly a portrait of the author as a young man: "His satirical sense kept him aloof. At first this was only a pose, and imitation of his father. But satire led to contempt," which "became part of his nature. It led to inadequacies, to self-awareness and a lasting loneliness. But it made him unassailable."

His fourth book, *A House for Mr. Biswas* is Naipaul's masterpiece. Alienation has not yet hardened into cynicism and condescension, and in creating a lightly fictionalized portrait of his father and his own childhood in Trinidad, Naipaul wrote about life in that Caribbean backwater with a mixture of sympathy and comic detachment. He used his journalist's eye for detail and his Dickensian gift for portraiture to give us an amazingly vivid sense of what it was like for Mr. Biswas, who lived in one room of a mud hut and worked as a sign painter, to aspire to the seemingly impossible quest of one day owning a house of his own—"on his own half-lot of land, his own portion of the earth." The house represents the dream of home and belonging, of achieving independence from his overbearing in-laws. And after years of working his way up to become a journalist and decades of mishaps and humiliations, Mr. Biswas does achieve this dream—before dying at the age of forty-six. Like Mr. Biswas, Naipaul's father, Seepersad, worked for a Trinidad newspaper; he was also an aspiring author, writing short stories "out of some private need." At some point, Seepersad transferred his literary dreams to his talented son, who, in turn, said he hoped his life might in some ways become a fulfillment of his father's. His dad, Naipaul wrote in 1983, was "a nibbler of books rather than a reader," but he "worshipped writing and writers. He made the vocation of the writer seem the noblest in the world; and I decided to be that noble thing."

BORN A CRIME
Stories from a South African Childhood

(2016)

Trevor Noah

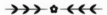

L ike his hosting of *The Daily Show,* Trevor Noah's stand-up comedy is fueled by his keen sense of the absurd— a knack honed, his compelling 2016 memoir, *Born a Crime,* makes clear, by his childhood in South Africa under apartheid.

By turns distressing, sad, and funny, his book provides an unnerving look, through the prism of his family, at recent South African history—the cruelties of daily life under that country's institutionalized racial segregation and white rule, and the country's lurching entry into a postapartheid era in the 1990s. Though some of his stories have a comic tone, they are raw, deeply personal reminiscences about being "half-white, half-black" in a country where his birth "violated any number of laws, statutes, and regulations."

The son of a Xhosa mother and a Swiss German father, Noah recalls that "the only time I could be with my father was indoors": "If we left the house, he'd have to walk across the street from us." It was dangerous, as a light-skinned child, to be seen with his mother as well: "She would hold my hand or carry me, but if the police showed up she would have to drop me and pretend I wasn't hers."

He spent much of his time at home: he didn't have friends and became good at being alone: "I'd read books, play with the toy that I had, make up imaginary worlds. I lived inside my head . . .

To this day you can leave me alone for hours and I'm perfectly happy entertaining myself. I have to remember to be with people."

Language, he discovered early, was a way to camouflage his difference. His mother knew Xhosa, Zulu, German, Afrikaans, and Sotho and used her knowledge "to cross boundaries, handle situations, navigate the world." She made sure that English was the first language her son spoke because "if you're black in South Africa, speaking English is the one thing that can give you a leg up."

A gifted mimic, Trevor learned to become "a chameleon," using language to gain acceptance in school and on the streets. "If you spoke to me in Zulu, I replied to you in Zulu," he writes. "If you spoke to me in Tswana, I replied to you in Tswana. Maybe I didn't look like you, but if I spoke like you, I was you." By high school, he had become an enterprising businessman, copying and selling pirated CDs. He and his friends would soon segue into the DJ business, throwing raucous dance parties in Alexandra, "a tiny, dense pocket of a shantytown," known as Gomorrah because it had "the wildest parties and the worst crimes."

BORN A CRIME *is not just a chilling account of growing up in South Africa under apartheid. It's also an eloquent love letter to the author's remarkable mother.*

Born a Crime is not just a chilling account of growing up in South Africa under apartheid. It's also an eloquent love letter to the author's remarkable mother, who grew up in a hut with fourteen cousins and determined that her son would not grow up paying what she called "the black tax"—black families having to "spend all of their time trying to fix the problems of the past," using their skills and education to bring their relatives "back up to zero," because "the generations who came before you have been pillaged."

It's the story of a fiercely religious woman who attributes her miraculous survival (from a gunshot wound to the head) to her faith; a woman who took her son to three churches on Sunday, as well as a prayer meeting on Tuesday, Bible study on Wednesday, and youth church on Thursday—even when there were dangerous riots in the streets and few dared to venture out of their homes.

The names chosen for Xhosa children traditionally have meanings, Noah writes. His mother's name, Patricia Nombuyiselo Noah, means "She Who Gives Back"; his cousin's name, Mlungisi, means "The Fixer." His mother, Noah adds, deliberately gave him a name, Trevor, with "no meaning whatsoever in South Africa, no precedent in my family": "It's not even a biblical name. It's just a name. My mother wanted her child beholden to no fate. She wanted me to be free to go anywhere, do anything, be anyone."

BOOKS BY BARACK OBAMA

DREAMS FROM MY FATHER: A Story of Race and Inheritance
(1995)

WE ARE THE CHANGE WE SEEK: The Speeches of Barack Obama
(2017) Edited by E. J. Dionne, Jr., and Joy-Ann Reid

→ ›› ❀ ‹‹ ←

Not since Lincoln has there been a president who has so powerfully used his eloquence as a writer—to inspire, to persuade, to articulate a vision—as Barack Obama. His most memorable speeches use the prism of history to amplify and crystallize the meaning of an occasion, reminding us of the ideals of liberty, justice, and equality that America was founded upon and the continuing, nearly two-and-a-half-century-long journey to make the promises of the Declaration of Independence real for everyone.

Like Lincoln and Martin Luther King, Jr., Obama has a long view of history; he sees the country as "a constant work in progress," a country scarred by the original sin of slavery but capable of overcoming the past through persistent work and dedication. And in his speeches, he reminds us how far America has come since the days of slavery and segregation, and how far we still have to go to create a more perfect union.

In his speech commemorating the fiftieth anniversary of the Selma to Montgomery march, President Obama argued that Selma is "not a museum or a static monument to behold from a distance"; rather, it's "one leg in our long journey toward freedom," an expression of "the belief that America is not yet finished, that we

DREAMS FROM MY FATHER

BARACK OBAMA

are strong enough to be self-critical, that each successive generation can look upon our imperfections and decide that it is in our power to remake this nation to more closely align with our highest ideals." It's an optimistic vision rooted in Scripture and its promise of redemption, and a more existential belief that people have the ability to continually remake themselves.

The searching intellect and gift for language that animate Obama's speeches as president were evident years before in the memoir *Dreams from My Father*, which he wrote when he was thirty-three. It's a memoir so affecting and fluently written that it's easy to imagine the young author choosing literature as a vocation instead of politics or law. The book attests to Obama's instinctive storytelling talents, his elastic voice as a writer, and that anomalous combination of empathy and detachment that gifted novelists and poets possess: an outsider's eye for the telling emotional detail, an aptitude for meditative reflection, and an ability to channel and give voice to the experiences of people he meets during his peripatetic youth and his years as a community organizer in Chicago.

The book tells the story of a young man's coming of age and his efforts to come to terms with the complexities of his racial identity, as the son of a father from Kenya (who left when he was a toddler) and a mother from Kansas. It's the story of the author's quest to understand his own family roots—a quest in which he cast himself as both a Telemachus in search of his father and an Odysseus in search of a home. The story of a boy who spent many of his formative years living with his maternal grandparents in Hawaii, grappling with fundamental questions of what he believed and where he belonged, talking with friends about race and identity, and reading books—by Baldwin, Ellison, Wright, Du Bois, Malcolm X— in an effort to try "to raise myself to be a black man in America."

In a preface to the 2004 edition of *Dreams from My Father,* Obama wrote that he hoped his own story "might speak in some way to the fissures of race that have characterized the American experience, as well as the fluid state of identity—the leaps through time, the collision of cultures—that mark our modern life." As he pointed out in the keynote address to the 2004 Democratic National Convention, the speech that first brought him to national attention, "In no other country on Earth is my story even possible."

THERE THERE

(2018)

Tommy Orange

*T*here *There,* the title of Tommy Orange's remarkable debut novel, comes from Gertrude Stein's famous line about Oakland, California—"There is no there there." For one of Orange's characters, Stein's observation about the Oakland she knew as a child having vanished is a metaphor for what happened to Native people all over America: their ancestral lands were stolen, sold, developed, paved over with "glass and concrete and wire and steel."

With *There There,* Orange—a member of the Cheyenne and Arapaho tribes of Oklahoma, and a recent graduate of the MFA program at the Institute of American Indian Arts—has written a symphonic novel about identity and the meaning of home, about families and memory and the power of storytelling. It's a novel that sweeps away all the stereotyped views of Native American lives that have been promoted by American culture for years—"the sad, defeated Indian silhouette," "Kevin Costner saving us, John Wayne's six-shooter slaying us—and gives us, instead, a kaleidoscopic look at contemporary Native American lives spanning three generations.

Writing in sharp, electric prose and cutting back and forth among a dozen points of view, Orange introduces us to a group of characters living in Oakland (or with roots there) whose interlinked lives will come crashing together at a big powwow held at the Oakland Coliseum. These people are trying to figure out who they are and where they belong, even what to call themselves.

"We didn't have last names before they came," Orange writes. "When they decided they needed to keep track of us, last names were given to us, just like the name *Indian* itself was given to us. These were attempted translations and botched Indian names, random surnames, and names passed down from white American generals, admirals, and colonels, and sometimes troop names, which were sometimes just colors. That's how we are Blacks and Browns, Greens, Whites, and Oranges. We are Smiths, Lees, Scotts, MacArthurs, Shermans, Johnsons, Jacksons. Our names are poems, descriptions of animals, images that make perfect sense and no sense at all."

Orvil Red Feather—who has been raised by his great-aunt, following the suicide of his mother—has learned most of what he knows "about being Indian" online, "googling stuff like 'What does it mean to be a real Indian.'" Thomas Frank—whose mom is white and whose dad is a "recovering alcoholic medicine man from the rez"—belongs to a drum group called Southern Moon, but he doesn't know how to deal with being mixed race: "You're from a people who took and took and took and took. And from a people taken. You were both and neither."

And Opal Viola Victoria Bear Shield—who has been raising her sister's three grandkids—recalls her mother telling her how important it was to remember the past, because the government was never going to make things right or even look back at what happened: "So what we could do had everything to do with being able to understand where we came from, what happened to our people, and how to honor them by living right, by telling our stories. She told me the world was made of stories, nothing else, just stories, and stories about stories."

Telling those stories, of course, is exactly what Tommy Orange has done in this fierce, sad, funny, and transcendent novel.

1984

(1949)

George Orwell

I n January 2017, the month Donald J. Trump was inaugurated as president, George Orwell's novel *1984* (first published in 1949) shot to the top of best-seller lists. Readers recognized that the dystopian novel—about a totalitarian state in which Big Brother uses lies, propaganda, and the sowing of hate to enforce the Party's absolute rule—held a frightening mirror to a political landscape increasingly filled with what Margaret Atwood once called Orwellian "danger flags."

The Trump administration has shamelessly used what one of the president's aides called "alternative facts" to defend its perverse decisions on everything from immigration policy to the reversing of regulations designed to protect the environment. Trump's barrage of lies, which continued to accelerate during his presidency, resembles the Kremlin's "firehose of falsehood" in Vladimir Putin's Russia: they not only promote misinformation, but are meant to foster the sort of numbness and cynicism that discourage people from caring about the political process.

During the first three years of Trump's presidency, many readers noticed other ominous echoes of *1984* as well: shameless appeals to fear and resentment (what Orwell described as daily "Two Minutes Hate" sessions) in an effort to divide the public; deliberate attempts to rewrite history and current events while denouncing the mainstream media as "fake news"; and the sidelining of science

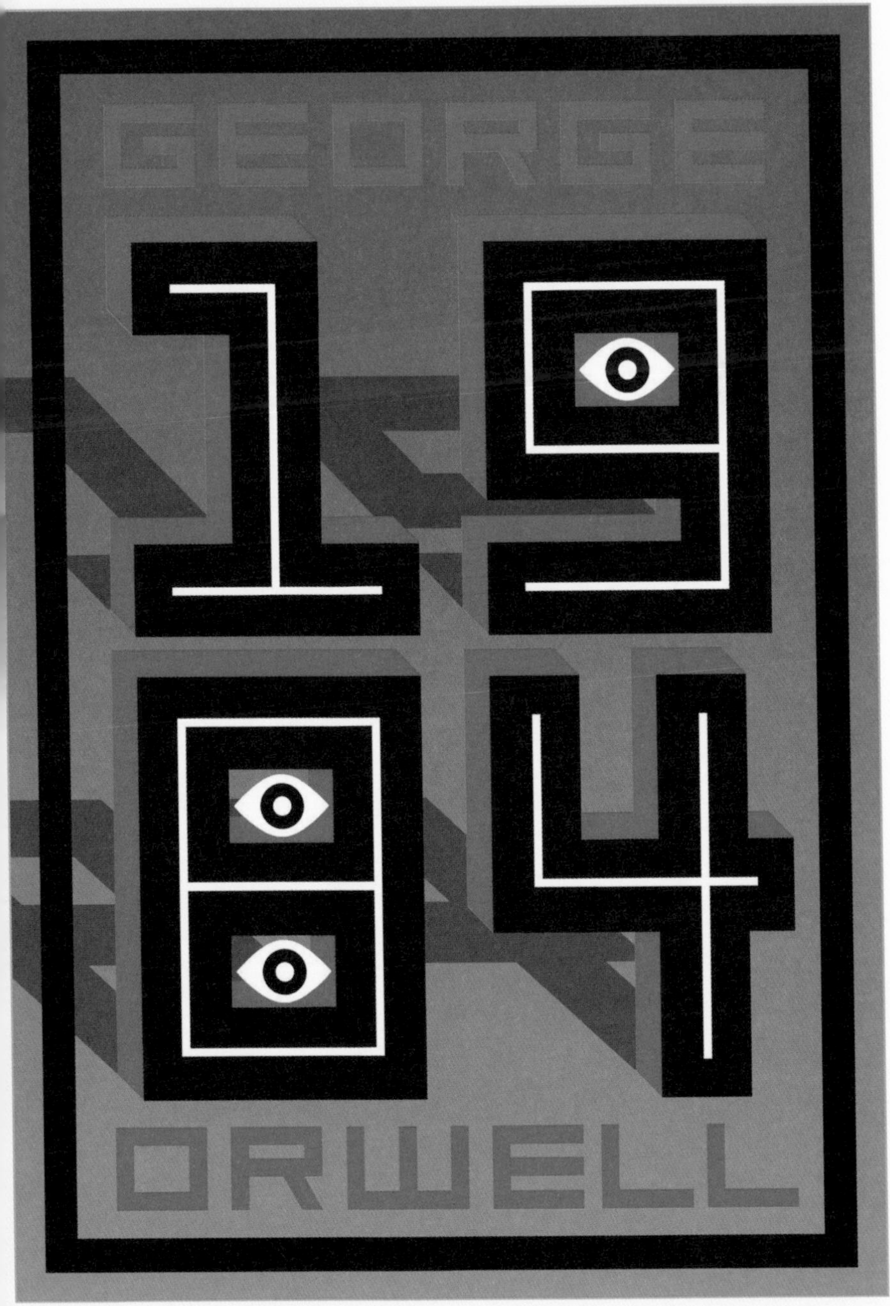
GEORGE
1984
ORWELL

and evidence-based arguments because such empirical methods of thought suggest, in Orwell's words, that "reality is something objective, external, existing in its own right." In *1984*, these are all tactics used by Big Brother to control the population, to insist that "whatever the Party holds to be truth, is truth"—even if it chooses to insist that "2 + 2 = 5" or that "war is peace," "freedom is slavery," and "ignorance is strength."

In a 1944 letter, Orwell explained why he was writing the novel that would become *1984*. He wrote that he was concerned about "the general indifference to the decay of democracy" and that he worried about the tendency of nationalistic movements "to group themselves round some superhuman fuhrer" and "to adopt the theory that the end justifies the means." With this, he added, came the proclivity "to disbelieve in the existence of objective truth because all the facts have to fit in with the words and prophecies" of one of these demagogic leaders.

Seven decades after the publication of *1984*, remarks made by President Trump and his enablers sound as if they were lifted from the pages of Orwell's classic.

"What you're seeing and what you're reading," Trump declared, "is not what's happening." His lawyer Rudolph Giuliani had these chilling words: "Truth isn't truth."

THE MOVIEGOER

(1961)

Walker Percy

Walker Percy's hero, Binx Bolling, has an affliction that will be instantly recognizable to people who are shy or sheltered or somehow dislocated and who spent a lot of time, when they were growing up, watching films or reading books: the stories Binx knows secondhand through movies often seem more real, more vivid than his own experiences.

As Binx explains, "Other people, so I have read, treasure memorable moments in their lives: the time one climbed the Parthenon at sunrise, the summer night one met a lonely girl in Central Park and achieved with her a sweet and natural relationship, as they say in books. I too once met a girl in Central Park, but it is not much to remember. What I remember is the time John Wayne killed three men with a carbine as he was falling to the dusty street in *Stagecoach,* and the time the kitten found Orson Welles in the doorway in *The Third Man.*"

Binx—a Korean War veteran and the scion of an aristocratic southern family—appears to lead a perfectly pleasant life in a middle-class New Orleans suburb where he works as a stock and bond trader. At twenty-nine, he is charming and witty and smart; he's had lots of girlfriends, drives a red MG, and spends his weekends on the Gulf Coast. Something is missing, however, and recalling an epiphany he had during the war, Binx decides to embark upon "a search." What exactly he's searching for isn't clear—purpose, maybe, or self-knowledge or faith—but he knows there has to be more to human existence than work and relaxation.

Binx is an emotional relative of sorts to Holden Caulfield in Salinger's *Catcher in the Rye* and to Joseph, the conflicted hero in Saul Bellow's *Dangling Man*—introspective protagonists in search of a way to live in a twentieth-century America that strikes them as phony, consumer oriented, and shallow. And like Holden, Binx proves to be an appealing narrator—someone we feel we've grown up with, an old, familiar friend. His chronic status as an observer will be familiar to many people today—even those not addicted to movies or books. After all, technology has increasingly insinuated itself between us and the world: we are often checking our phones for texts or emails, instead of paying attention to the people around us.

Although *The Moviegoer* was his first published novel, Percy had been writing essays for years—inspired by all the philosophy books he'd been reading while recuperating from tuberculosis he'd contracted after finishing medical school. And the ideas of Søren Kierkegaard, and to a lesser extent Camus and Sartre, percolate through *The Moviegoer* and such later Percy novels as *The Last Gentleman* and *Lancelot*. Binx himself uses lots of philosophical terms to try to explain his efforts to find himself, talking about reading important books—like *War and Peace* and Schrödinger's *What Is Life?*—as part of his "vertical search" to understand the universe.

The reader gradually realizes, however, that Binx's lofty talk about such matters is actually part of his detachment from the world—and his need to intellectualize every aspect of his daily life. After Binx's aunt asks him to keep an eye on a distant cousin named Kate—who's had suicidal impulses—Binx stops talking about his search. He slowly falls in love with the vulnerable Kate, and in caring for her, he takes a step outside himself and steps out into the world.

MASON & DIXON

(1997)

Thomas Pynchon

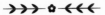

A nearly eight-hundred-page buddy novel about two eighteenth-century surveyors might not sound like the most compelling proposition, but in his brilliant 1997 novel, *Mason & Dixon,* Thomas Pynchon turned this premise into the most affecting and immersive novel of his career, and a profoundly inventive meditation on American history and its costs and discontents.

Mason and Dixon, of course, are the real-life British surveyors who mapped out the boundary line between Pennsylvania and Maryland in pre-Revolutionary America—the line that would come to be known as the Mason-Dixon Line, dividing the North from the South. As Pynchon tells it, Mason, who had trained as an astronomer, is the melancholy one: brooding, solitary, and haunted by the death of his wife. Dixon is the gregarious one: fond of women and drink and a good time.

In Pynchon's antic reimagining of their story, they become as memorable a pair as Don Quixote and Sancho Panza, Tom and Huck, Bing Crosby and Bob Hope. And their quest to chart the wilderness supplies Pynchon with an armature for his ebullient picaresque tale: a kind of Christmas tree he can festoon with jokes, songs, puns, satiric vaudeville turns, and meandering, Tristram Shandy–like digressions about everything from a mechanical duck, to a giant cheese, to the transits of Venus.

Pynchon injects his early America with a darkly comic metaphysics reminiscent of that in his 1966 novel, *The Crying of Lot 49*. At the same time, the world he's created here possesses a kind of small-town intimacy that will remind some readers of Larry McMurtry's West.

As depicted by Pynchon, Mason and Dixon's quest to draw their line through the wilderness becomes a metaphor for the efforts made by the founding generation to build a new nation based on the Enlightenment principles of reason and progress. A nation dedicated to the democratic ideals of freedom and equality and yet settled and built with untold violence and exploitation: the massacre of Indians, the buying and selling of slaves, the domestication of a wilderness of possibilities and its transformation into a numbing landscape of "Inns and Shops, Stables, Games of Skill, Theatrickals, Pleasure-Gardens . . . a Promenade,—nay, Mall."

Pynchon's favorite themes twine their way through this novel, most notably the dynamic between order and chaos, destiny and free choice, paranoia and nihilism. Are there far-fetched conspiracies that explain the complexities of the universe, or are things merely random? Do the strange coincidences that seem to proliferate in modern life signify a hidden design, or are they simply reflections of our obsessive need to connect the dots; to create narratives and stories; to map, as it were, the uncharted wilderness?

All of Pynchon's signature gifts as a storyteller are on ample display here—including his penchant for shaggy-dog plotlines, his fondness for ditzy, Dickensian names, and his magpie talents as a storyteller—but he has never before created characters with the emotional depth of Mason and Dixon. Indeed this novel opens out into a grand meditation on American history while at the same time disclosing the inner lives of its heroes with elegiac sympathy and wisdom.

LIFE

(2010)

Keith Richards (with James Fox)

For legions of Rolling Stones fans, Keith Richards is not only the heart and soul of the world's greatest rock-and-roll band; he's also the very avatar of rebellion: the desperado, the buccaneer, the *poète maudit,* the soul survivor and main offender, the torn and frayed outlaw, and the coolest dude on the planet, named both No. 1 on the rock stars most-likely-to-die list and the one life-form (besides the cockroach) capable of surviving nuclear war.

In his electrifying memoir, *Life,* Richards writes about the weirdness of being mythologized by fans as a sort of folk-hero renegade and chronicles the exhausting rituals of life on the road and the magic of writing and recording new music in the studio.

By turns earnest and wicked, sweet and sarcastic and unsparing, Richards writes with uncommon immediacy and candor. He gives us an indelible, time-capsule feel for the madness that was life on the road with the Stones in the years before and after Altamont; unnerving accounts of the author's many close shaves and narrow escapes (from the police, prison time, heroin addiction); and a deck of sharp-edged snapshots of friends and colleagues.

But *Life* is way more than a revealing showbiz memoir. It is also a high-def, high-velocity portrait of the era when rock and roll came of age, a raw report from deep inside the counterculture maelstrom of how that music swept like a tsunami over Britain

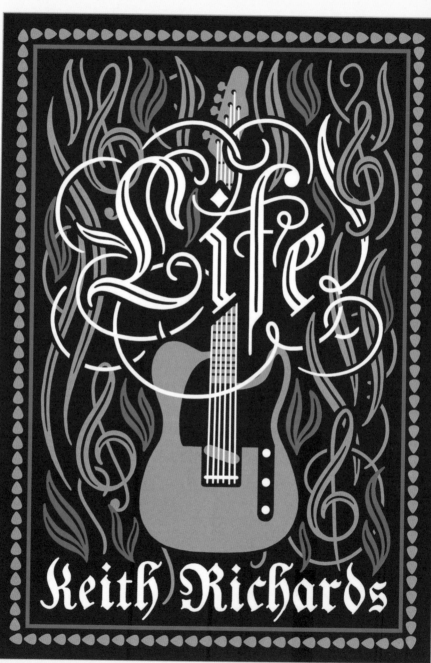

and the United States. It's an eye-opening all-nighter in the studio with a master craftsman disclosing the alchemical secrets of his art. And it's the intimate and moving story of one man's long strange trip over the decades, told without any of the pretense, caution, or self-consciousness that usually attends great artists sitting for their self-portraits.

Die-hard Stones fans, of course, will pore over the detailed discussions of how songs like "Ruby Tuesday" and "Gimme Shelter" came to be written, the birthing process of some of Richards's classic guitar riffs, and the collaborative dynamic between him and Mick Jagger. But the book will also dazzle the uninitiated who thought they had only a casual interest in the Stones or who viewed Richards, vaguely, as a rock god who was mad, bad, and dangerous to know. The book is that compelling.

Richards's prose is like his guitar playing: intense, elemental, utterly distinctive, and achingly, emotionally direct. Just as the Stones perfected a signature sound that could accommodate everything from ferocious Dionysian anthems to melancholy ballads about love and time and loss, so Richards has found a voice in these pages— a kind of rich, primal Keith-Speak—that enables him to dispense funny, streetwise observations, tender family reminiscences, casually profane yarns, and wry literary allusions with both heartfelt sincerity and bad-boy charm.

Songwriting, Richards says, long ago turned him into an observer always on the lookout for "ammo," and he does a highly tactile job here of conjuring the past, whether he's describing his post–World War II childhood in the little town of Dartford, the smoky blues clubs that he and his friends haunted in their early days in London, or the wretched excess of the Stones' later tours, when they had "become a pirate nation," booking entire floors in hotels and "moving on a huge scale under our own flag, with lawyers, clowns, attendants."

Richards communicates the boyish astonishment he felt when the Stones found their dream of being missionaries for the American music they loved suddenly giving way to pop fame of their own and their hand-to-mouth existence in a London tenement (financed in part by redeeming empty beer bottles stolen from parties) metamorphosed into full-on stardom, complete with rioting teenagers and screaming girls, pharmaceutical cocaine, and impulsive jaunts abroad ("let's jump in the Bentley and go to Morocco").

But the most insistent melodic line in this volume has nothing to do with drugs or celebrity or scandal. It has to do with the sponge-like love of music Richards inherited from his grandfather and his own sense of musical history, his reverence for the blues and R&B masters he has studied his entire life ("the tablets of stone"), and his determination to pass his own knowledge on down the line.

One of this galvanic book's many achievements is that Richards has found a way to channel to the reader his own passion for music, and to make us feel the connections that bind one generation of musicians to another. Along the way he even manages to communicate something of that magic, electromagnetic experience of playing onstage with his mates, be it in a little club or a huge stadium. "There's a certain moment when you realize that you've actually just left the planet for a bit and that nobody can touch you," Richards writes. "You're elevated because you're with a bunch of guys that want to do the same thing as you. And when it works, baby, you've got wings." You are, he says, "flying without a license."

A LIFE OF PICASSO

THE PRODIGY, 1881–1906 (1991)

THE CUBIST REBEL, 1907–1916 (1996)

THE TRIUMPHANT YEARS, 1917–1932 (2007)

John Richardson

Talking about his own highly eclectic, highly protean style, Pablo Picasso once said to his mistress Françoise Gilot, "Of course if you note all the different shapes, sizes, and colors of models he works from, you can understand his confusion. He doesn't know what he wants. No wonder his style is so ambiguous. It's like God's. God is really only another artist. He invented the giraffe, the elephant, and the cat. He has no real style. He just keeps on trying other things. The same with this sculptor. First he works from nature; then he tries abstraction. Finally he winds up lying around caressing his models."

The comparison to God, like the use of the third person, was deliberate, of course. As the art historian and curator John Richardson reminds us in his magisterial multivolume biography, Picasso was not only a prodigal artistic genius but also a self-mythologizing Minotaur who believed that he could redefine the universe with his daring and his talent. He was a Nietzschean shaman who regarded art as a mysterious, magical force, offering the possibility of exorcism and transfiguration; a chameleon who effortlessly moved back and forth between cubism and classicism, irony and sentimentality, cruelty and tenderness; a wily, cannibalistic sorcerer who inhaled history, ideas, and a vast array of styles with fierce, promiscuous abandon—all toward the end of exploding convention and making the world anew.

In volume 1, Richardson—who was a friend and neighbor of Picasso's in the South of France—provides a detailed history of the artist's family and his precocious childhood, authoritatively peeling away the myths, rumors, and speculation that have accreted, like layers of varnish, around the man.

Volume 2 is centered on cubism, the movement Picasso founded with Georges Braque, a movement, in Richardson's view, that nourished Picasso's later achievements and also fueled "every major modernist movement" that followed. Chronicling the genesis and evolution of cubism, Richardson deftly explains how its fracturing of reality and manipulation of multiple viewpoints resulted in an art that was simultaneously representational and anti-naturalistic, an earthy revolt against the pretty, surface-shimmer of impressionism. He argues that the first phase of cubism, which enabled its practitioners to take things apart like surgeons, made possible the later achievements of de Stijl, constructivism, and minimalism. Its second phase, he writes, enabled followers to put things back together again and laid the groundwork for the dadaists, the surrealists, and even the pop artists.

Richardson, who died at the age of ninety-five in 2019, did not complete volume 4, the final installment of Picasso's life, but volume 3 takes us on an enthralling tour through the artist's mid-career peregrinations. Richardson sketches out the competitive dialogue that Picasso carried on for years with Matisse, and maps the myriad intramural spats and schisms that fractured the art world during the opening decades of the twentieth century.

Even if Picasso is not your favorite artist, it's impossible not to be fascinated by how his bravura, sometimes violent work revolutionized modern art, how it altered the very vocabulary of painting and seeing. And there is no one to explain it with more authority and panache than Richardson, whose consummate knowledge of Picasso's work is on display throughout these books—from his insights into the artist's temperament and sources of inspiration, to his understanding of the sorcery by which Picasso transformed his own experiences and emotions into art. With his incisive and revealing commentaries on individual artworks and his tracing of larger dynamics in Picasso's career, Richardson leaves us with a deep appreciation of the artist's Promethean ambition and prodigious fecundity, and a shrewd understanding of the cultural legacy left by his tumultuous, subversive work.

Picasso once observed that his work was a kind of diary of his life, and in this biography Richardson expertly translates that journal, showing us how the artist's homes and surroundings surfaced in his work, how his competitive study of other painters' work informed particular canvases and sketches, how his feelings toward the women in his life—passion, rage, resentment—surfaced in his imagery, from doves and stringed instruments, to hideously distorted biomorphic shapes.

As in Ovid's poems, the idea of transformation became a metaphor for the chaotic, unpredictable nature of the world. Violent change and transmogrification became the means by which Picasso could use his voracious visual memory and digestive powers to assimilate the work of other artists, Richardson suggests, and, by reinventing their idioms and images, somehow triumph over them—to show, in his magical and warlike view of art, that he possessed them, possessed the past, and was steering history in a new, modernist direction.

"I am God," Picasso once told a Spanish friend. "I am God. I am God."

BOOKS ABOUT WORK
AND VOCATION

SICK IN THE HEAD: Conversations About Life and Comedy (2015)
Judd Apatow

THE RIGHT KIND OF CRAZY: A True Story of Teamwork,
Leadership, and High-Stakes Innovation (2016)
Adam Steltzner (with William Patrick)

THE SHEPHERD'S LIFE: Modern Dispatches from
an Ancient Landscape (2015)
James Rebanks

DO NO HARM: Stories of Life, Death, and Brain Surgery (2014)
Henry Marsh

Expertise is mesmerizing—whether it's Steph Curry sinking one
amazing clutch three after another from virtually every spot on the
court, Aretha Franklin investing every classic she sang with her
own mystery and magic, or Mikhail Baryshnikov reinventing the
possibilities of dance with his extraordinary ability to combine
athleticism and artistry.

We want to understand how people practice and hone their craft—
the knowledge, techniques, and skill they bring to their vocations. As
Studs Terkel's Working *reminded us many years ago, work consumes*
many hours of our days, and particularly for those fortunate enough

to have jobs they find meaningful, it can provide a revealing window through which to view the world.

Here are several books in which authors write eloquently about their professions, giving us an insider's appreciation of the know-how behind their craft—the underwater part of the iceberg, so to speak—and the rituals and routines and years of practice and apprenticeship that went into learning proficiency and, in time, mastery and finesse.

J udd Apatow was a comedy freak as long as he can remember. Growing up, he circled the names of comedians in *TV Guide* so he wouldn't miss one of their appearances on a talk show. When he was in the fifth grade, he wrote a thirty-page report on the lives and careers of the Marx Brothers—not even for a class, but for his "own personal use." And in tenth grade, he started interviewing comedians—like Jerry Seinfeld, John Candy, Harold Ramis, Jay Leno—for his high school radio station. Since then, of course, Apatow has become a comedy legend himself—executive producer of *Freaks and Geeks* and *Girls* and writer and director of such hit movies as *The 40-Year-Old Virgin, Knocked Up, Funny People, This Is 40*, and *The King of Staten Island*. He's also continued to interview comedians—artists who are now longtime friends and colleagues. He's collected those interviews in *Sick in the Head*—a book that's a wonderful oral history of comedy and a revealing look at the art of comedy, as practiced by the likes of Mel Brooks, Mike Nichols, Steve Martin, Chris Rock, Jon Stewart, Amy Schumer, Stephen Colbert, and Sarah Silverman.

Apatow is a terrific interviewer, and his subjects are far more spontaneous and forthcoming than they are with many journalists. In the early interviews, they give the young Apatow—a highly informed fanboy who seems to know their work as well as they do—concrete and helpful advice about writing and performing, as well as a real appreciation of the patience and self-knowledge required to find a voice of one's own. The later interviews are actually conversations between friends and fellow practitioners of an art form who talk—often with startling emotional candor and wisdom—about everything from the childhood traumas that led them to comedy in the first place, to the relationship between their real-life selves and the characters they create on paper and on the stage and screen.

Garry Shandling—the subject of Apatow's Emmy Award–winning 2018 documentary, *The Zen Diaries of Garry Shandling,* and the 2019 book *It's Garry Shandling's Book*—taught the young Apatow, whom he'd hired as a writer on *The Larry Sanders Show,* that the key in storytelling was "to try to get to the emotional core of each character" and that "comedy is about truth and revealing yourself."

As Shandling put it, "The most important thing a comic can do is write from his insides. As cliché as that sounds, a lot of comics start out thinking that they just should write something funny. Which is not the answer. You have to write from personal experience."

Apatow and many of his colleagues speak at length about what they learned from their comedy heroes. In fact, there is a sense of fraternity throughout this book, a sense of how one artist, one generation, passes on lessons and inspiration to the next. "My whole life I'd wanted friends who had similar interests and a similar worldview," Apatow writes, "people I could talk with about Monty

Python and *SCTV*. People who could recite every line on the *Let's Get Small* album and who knew who George Carlin's original comedy team partner was (Jack Burns). It was lonely having this interest that no one shared." He found those friends in the people interviewed in these pages, and in writing the book, he passes on to readers honorary membership in what he calls "the tribe of comedians."

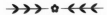

When the Mars rover Curiosity stuck its landing on the red planet on August 6, 2012, it opened a new era in space exploration, and it also signified a triumph of human ingenuity over staggering odds. There was virtually zero margin of error with the $2.5 billion project, and any number of things could have gone wrong with a mission that depended upon the work of more than seven thousand scientists and engineers and about 500,000 lines of computer code.

After being blasted into space by an Atlas V rocket on November 26, 2011, Curiosity spent eight months hurtling some 354 million miles through space, plunging into Mars's atmosphere at a brutal 13,200 miles an hour. For the rover to alight safely in the chosen landing zone, the entire process of entry, descent, and landing had to work perfectly. That process involved rocket-powered deceleration, a giant parachute, and a sky crane using nylon ropes to lower Curiosity gently onto the surface of Mars and set it directly down on its wheels.

In *The Right Kind of Crazy*, Adam Steltzner, an engineer who headed up the NASA team in charge of that landing, recounts just how that remarkable feat was pulled off, leaving us with an appreciation of the technical knowledge and in-the-moment skills that team members possessed. He provides an understanding of the hard data, intuition, and around-the-clock work involved in the project, and the way engineers learned to break down seemingly impossible problems into smaller, more manageable ones that they could "egghead" their way through.

On top of racing the clock, which had been "set by celestial mechanics" (that is, the movements of Earth and Mars in the sky), Steltzner's team was faced with inventing a landing system for the car-sized Curiosity, which was filled with delicate scientific equipment and way too heavy for the air-bag cocoons used in earlier rover missions.

Happily, the landing worked as planned. For almost eight years now, the little rover has been working diligently, trundling across the surface of the red planet, looking for evidence that the planet could have once supported life, and sending home massive amounts of data and photos, and the occasional tweet. On the first anniversary of its safe landing on Mars, hundreds of millions of miles from Earth, the lonely little rover sang "Happy Birthday" to itself.

In his captivating book, *The Shepherd's Life*, James Rebanks tells us about the small sheep farm in England's Lake District that's been in his family for generations. His story is one about tradition and roots in an age of change and flux; belonging in an era of transience. He describes the seasonal rhythms of farm life: clipping the sheep in the summer and stockpiling hay for the winter; bringing the sheep down from higher ground in the autumn; and preparing for lambing time in the spring. He describes the exhausting, repetitive tasks that define farm life—mending walls, chopping logs, moving flocks between fields. And he communicates an intimate sense of the knowledge that his family and their neighbors have of their land: "We see a thousand shades of green, like the Inuit see different kinds of snow."

What shines throughout the book is Rebanks's love of his work— "If I had only a few days left on earth," he writes, "I would spend one of them inspecting Herdwick" rams—and his knowledge that the lives of his family are "entwined around something we all cared about more than anything else in the world. The farm."

I n *Do No Harm,* Henry Marsh, one of Britain's foremost neurosurgeons, gives readers an extraordinarily intimate, compassionate, and sometimes frightening understanding of his vocation—a profession he compares to bomb disposal work, "though the bravery required is of a different kind as it is the patient's life that is at risk and not the surgeon's."

There was the thrill of "the chase," as the surgeon stalked his prey deep within the brain, then "the climax, as he caught the aneurysm, trapped it, and obliterated it with a glittering, spring-loaded titanium clip, saving the patient's life." More than that, Marsh goes on, "the operation involved the brain, the mysterious substrate of all thought and feeling, of all that was important in human life—a mystery, it seemed to me, as great as the stars at night and the universe around us. The operation was elegant, delicate, dangerous and full of profound meaning."

When he was younger, Marsh recalls, he used to feel an "intense exhilaration" after a successful operation; he felt, he says, "like a conquering general," having averted disaster and safely delivered his patient: "It was a deep and profound feeling which I suspect few people other than surgeons ever get to experience." But while he's saved many patients, he remains haunted by those surgeries that failed—the headstones in "that cemetery which the French surgeon Leriche once said all surgeons carry within themselves."

Marsh writes about the complicated calculus of risk that surgeons must make, weighing the possibility of saving patients from slow deterioration or constant pain against the danger of making them worse. He writes about "surgical stage fright" and his distaste for seeing patients on the morning of their operations, and how those anxieties give way to "fierce and happy concentration" once he is in the operating room.

However much Marsh may talk about the detachment that doctors must learn, this book underscores how much he cares for his patients. Many of the most difficult moments he recounts take place not in the operating room but in conversations before or after surgery— conversations in which Marsh tries to balance realism (the knowledge that "they are being stalked by death") with his patients' need for hope, "that fragile beam of light in so much darkness."

HOUSEKEEPING

(1980)

Marilynne Robinson

Marilynne Robinson's beautiful debut novel, *Housekeeping*, is a haunting story about familial love and loss and the impermanence of life. It's also a novel that pivots around that central tension in American literature—from Mark Twain through Jack Kerouac, John Updike, and Sam Shepard—between roots and rootlessness, domesticity and freedom, the safety of home and the exhilaration of the road.

Housekeeping is narrated by Ruth, who—much like Scout in *To Kill a Mockingbird*—is looking back on her small-town girlhood. Ruth and her sister, Lucille, were young children when their mother, Helen, dropped them at their grandmother's house, then drove a friend's Ford off the top of a cliff, into the depths of a remote Idaho lake—the same lake that, years before, had claimed the life of her father and many others, when the engine of their train somehow slid off the local bridge, pulling the rest of the railroad cars after it into the water.

For five years, Ruthie and Lucille were well cared for by their grandmother, but when she died, they were turned over to relatives, who didn't particularly want to parent two orphans and who somehow talked their mysterious aunt Sylvie into moving back to the town of Fingerbone.

Sylvie, we learn, has spent years as a drifter, moving from town to town, and she's clearly something of an eccentric—ill-disposed toward regular routines or ordinary housekeeping, at least as practiced by the nice middle-class folks in 1950s Fingerbone. Sylvie eats graham crackers and Cheerios instead of real meals, lets old newspapers pile up around the house, likes to sit alone in the dark. Sylvie was "like a mermaid in a ship's cabin," Ruthie remembers. "She preferred it sunk in the very element it was meant to exclude. We had crickets in the pantry, squirrels in the eaves, sparrows in the attic."

The sisters initially worry that Sylvie will abandon them, as their mother did, and Lucille comes to resent Sylvie's unconventional ways; she wants a normal life, she says, a life like everyone else's. When the neighbors and town authorities start questioning Sylvie's parenting and housekeeping skills, she and Ruthie devise a plan that will enable them to stay together as a family. Like Huck Finn, they have had it with being "sivilized"; they want to "light out for the Territory" and hit the road.

Robinson has written about studying Emerson and the transcendentalists, and in some ways *Housekeeping* is a dramatization of the central ideas that Emerson explored in "Self-Reliance"— the famous essay in which he argued that individuals should strive for independence, spurn conformity and the expectations of others, and embrace solitude as a path to self-knowledge. But *Housekeeping* is in no way didactic; it's both a deeply affecting and gently comic portrait of a fractured family and a lyrical prose poem that has the spiritual transparency of a harpsichord solo and the high, lonesome melody of a bluegrass ballad.

AMERICAN PASTORAL

(1997)

Philip Roth

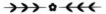

After years of complicating his own life on paper, Philip
Roth put aside the mirror games in his 1997 novel,
American Pastoral, and instead tackled the social, political,
and cultural complexities of American history. The result was the
most expansive and resonant novel of his career—a book that
used the prism of one family's travails to examine what happened
to America in the decades between World War II and Vietnam,
between the complacencies of the 1950s and the confusions of the
1960s, '70s, and '80s.

In a 1961 (1961!) essay, Roth argued that American life was
becoming so strange and surreal that it had ceased to be a
manageable subject for novelists, that real-life stories in the
headlines had surpassed the imaginings of fiction writers, goading
authors like himself to abandon "the grander social and political
phenomena of our times" in favor of works focused on the more
knowable world of the self.

American Pastoral burst through such inhibitions with astonishing
verve. In exploring the intersection between the personal and the
political, it turned the generational struggles that afflict so many Roth
characters into a kind of parable about two contradictory impulses
in American history: the first, embodied by his hero Seymour Levov,
representing that optimistic strain of Emersonian self-reliance
predicated upon a belief in hard work and progress; the second,

embodied by the Swede's rebellious daughter, Merry, representing the darker side of American individualism, what Roth called "the fury, the violence, and the desperation" of "the indigenous American berserk."

In earlier Roth novels like *Portnoy's Complaint,* the collision of the prudent and the transgressive, the ordinary and the Dionysian, was the source of uproarious comedy. But in *American Pastoral,* that same clash generates a familial showdown with tragic consequences—one that becomes a kind of metaphor for the schisms within American culture that broke open in the 1960s and have since festered and deepened.

As a young man, Seymour seemed like the all-American golden boy: earnest, athletic, reliable. After high school, he became a Marine, married Miss New Jersey of 1949, and took over his father's glove business. During the height of anti–Vietnam War protests, however, his life abruptly shatters when his daughter, Merry, sets off a bomb that kills a man in a small-town post office.

How did Merry metamorphose, virtually overnight, from a girl who loved astronomy and Audrey Hepburn into a violent left-wing activist? Like her father, the reader struggles to make sense of her life, struggles to explain how this cherished daughter of privileged parents could end up a fugitive from justice—a young woman described as "chaos itself." That is one of Roth's points in this powerful novel—that events are not rational, that life is not coherent, that the old certainties of the American dream often come flying apart when hit by one of the curveballs thrown by history.

THE HARRY POTTER NOVELS

HARRY POTTER AND THE PHILOSOPHER'S STONE (1997)

HARRY POTTER AND THE CHAMBER OF SECRETS (1998)

HARRY POTTER AND THE PRISONER OF AZKABAN (1999)

HARRY POTTER AND THE GOBLET OF FIRE (2000)

HARRY POTTER AND THE ORDER OF THE PHOENIX (2003)

HARRY POTTER AND THE HALF-BLOOD PRINCE (2005)

HARRY POTTER AND THE DEATHLY HALLOWS (2007)

J. K. Rowling

With her seven *Harry Potter* novels written over a decade, J. K. Rowling has created a fictional world as meticulously detailed and fully imagined as Oz or Narnia or Middle-earth—a world with its own rules and traditions and history. Although Rowling grounds Harry's story in the mundane Muggle world, where he undergoes all the frustrations and challenges of ordinary adolescence, she uses her endlessly inventive imagination to conjure a magical realm where owls deliver messages, paintings can talk, and the return of a Luciferian dark lord threatens the future of the free world.

Each volume grows progressively darker as Harry prepares for his ultimate confrontation with Lord Voldemort. Quidditch games give way to Defence Against the Dark Arts training, and magic,

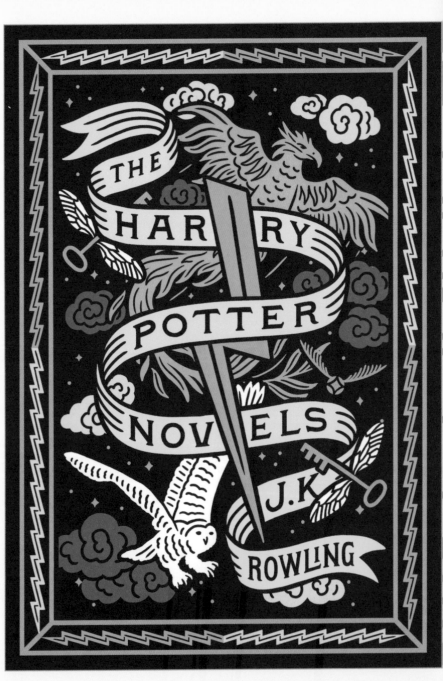

THE HARRY POTTER NOVELS

J.K. ROWLING

once the subject of Hogwarts classes, is now a weapon of war. More and more responsibilities are heaped on Harry's shoulders as he becomes the leader of the Resistance against Voldemort. By the final installment of the series, he is more Henry V than Prince Hal, more King Arthur than young Wart.

Rowling moves Harry's story forward through a series of challenges and tests, even as she uses flashbacks to move backward in time. Indeed Harry's growing emotional wisdom is rooted in his understanding of the past, both that of his own family and that of Hogwarts and the ancient world of wizarding.

Already an orphan, Harry loses his surrogate fathers—Dumbledore and Sirius—and he is haunted by the knowledge that he has a strange psychic connection with Voldemort. He must enter a dark wood where he does battle not only with the Dark Lord but also with the temptations of hubris and despair.

The Potter books are deeply rooted in traditional literature and big-screen epics—from ancient Greek and Norse myths to Tolkien and C. S. Lewis to *Star Wars*; from Homer's *Iliad* and Milton's *Paradise Lost* to T. H. White's *The Once and Future King* and the comic book and movie versions of *Spider-Man*. But Rowling has transformed her love of the classics into an epic that transcends its sources as effortlessly as it leapfrogs conventional genres—the coming-of-age novel, the detective story, the family saga, and folktales about heroes who redeem their endangered homelands. In doing so, she created a series of books that not only captivate both children and adults but also underscore the cultural power of YA fiction and the fantasy genre, helped turn millennials into a generation of avid readers, and changed the dynamics of fandom. They are novels that constitute one of literature's ultimate bildungsromans and that hold a mirror to our own mortal world as it lurches into the uncertainties of the twenty-first century.

BOOKS BY SALMAN RUSHDIE

MIDNIGHT'S CHILDREN (1981)

THE MOOR'S LAST SIGH (1995)

S
alman Rushdie's bravura 1981 novel, *Midnight's Children,*
and its 1995 bookend, *The Moor's Last Sigh,* are both surreal
parables about Indian history since independence—its bright
hopes spiraling downward into the disillusion that accompanied the
emergency measures imposed by Prime Minister Indira Gandhi in
1975, as early dreams of pluralism gave way to sectarian violence
and political corruption.

They are novels that showcase Rushdie's gifts as a writer and
the ambitious themes that fuel his most powerful fiction: a restless
and inventive imagination, deployed in the service of mapping the
history of the Indian subcontinent; exuberant, fevered language, by
turns high-flown and streetwise, comic and elegiac; and a visceral
understanding of the cultural and psychological sense of exile
created by the shifting tectonics of history.

In *Midnight's Children,* India's fate was incarnated in the lives
of 1,001 children born during the first hour of Indian independence
(that moment when "clock-hands joined palms in respectful
greeting"), whose destinies will be "indissolubly chained" to that of
their country. Each of these children possesses magical, idiosyncratic
gifts—like the ability to travel through time, or see the future—but
they will end up being drained of hope.

The book's narrator, Saleem, who possesses the gift of telepathy,
was supposedly born into a wealthy Muslim family, but he will

 *The narrators are modern-day Scheherazades who share their creator's love and reverence for storytelling and who spin history and their own lives into myth.*

later learn that a nurse switched him at birth with Shiva, now the son of an impoverished Hindu street singer. Saleem and Shiva will become archenemies, and their bitter rivalry will help undermine the promise of the rest of midnight's children.

In *The Moor's Last Sigh,* the subcontinent's fate is similarly embodied in the ups and downs of the sprawling da Gama–Zogoiby family, and more specifically in the adventures of the clan's last surviving member, Moraes Zogoiby, otherwise known as Moor.

Moor is a bastard child who suffers from a rare genetic disorder that causes him to age at twice the usual rate, and he, too, becomes an emblematic figure who shares India's plight—the plight of a country forced to grow up too quickly, "without time for proper planning," without time to learn from experience, "without time for reflection."

In fact, Moor's entire family is riven by jealousies, betrayals, and terrible acts of vengeance. Two sides of his mother's family battled each other for years before a division of the house and family business was decreed; another family standoff pitted a brother who was a committed nationalist against a brother who was pro-British. The romance between Moor's Catholic mother and his Jewish father nearly ended in a Romeo-Juliet debacle. And his great-grandmother died with a curse on her lips: "May your house be for ever partitioned, may its foundations turn to dust, may your children rise up against you, and may your fall be hard."

It is a curse that Moor will live to see fulfilled as he is forced to choose between his possessive mother's dream of a pluralistic India and his passionate girlfriend's vision of religious absolutism; between his father's world of violence and money and his own world of words and art. By the end of the book, after many murders, many fights, many tirades and schemes and disasters, the da Gama–Zogoiby family is in ruins, as is Bombay, leaving Moor, after his fall from grace and banishment, alone to tell the tale.

The narrators of *Midnight's Children* and *The Moor's Last Sigh* are both modern-day Scheherazades who share their creator's love and reverence for storytelling and who spin history and their own lives into myth. In his 2012 memoir, *Joseph Anton,* Rushdie wrote of feeling privileged to be a practitioner of "the beautiful, ancient art" of storytelling, and described how literature encourages "understanding, sympathy, and identification with people not like oneself," at a time when "the world was pushing everyone in the opposite direction, toward narrowness, bigotry, tribalism, cultism and war."

BOOKS BY OLIVER SACKS

THE MAN WHO MISTOOK HIS WIFE FOR A HAT,
AND OTHER CLINICAL TALES (1985)

AN ANTHROPOLOGIST ON MARS: Seven Paradoxical Tales (1995)

Oliver Sacks

The gifts that made Oliver Sacks an extraordinary writer are the same qualities that made him an ideal doctor: deep reserves of empathy, keen powers of observation, and an intuitive understanding of the mysteries of the human mind. In books like *The Man Who Mistook His Wife for a Hat* and *An Anthropologist on Mars,* he celebrated the symmetries and strange and wonderful interconnectedness of life—between the body and the mind, science and art, the beauty of the natural world and the magic of the human imagination.

His portraits of patients in these books are so unexpected and so resonant that they read like tales by Borges or Calvino. Dr. P., a music teacher, finds his visual and perceptual abilities so impaired that he mistakes his wife's head for a hat and can identify a rose only as "a convoluted red form with a linear green attachment." Twins named John and Michael dwell in a mental landscape composed entirely of numbers: while they have difficulty with the most mundane of daily tasks, they can instantly memorize sequences of three hundred digits and rattle off twenty-digit primes without a pause. One man, reminiscent of Borges's Funes the Memorious, obsessively remembers everything about his youth in a small

Italian village and seems incapable of thinking about anything else. Another man possesses a memory that's stopped in the 1960s, imprisoning him in a time capsule defined by early rock and roll.

Sacks wrote about such people not as patients suffering from a crippling loss or affliction but as individuals whose dilemmas—psychological, moral, and spiritual—become as real to us as those of characters by Chekhov or William Trevor. He was concerned with the impact that their neurological disorders had on their relationships, their day-to-day routines, and the landscape of their imaginations. His case studies became literary narratives that underscored not the marginality of his patients' experiences but their part in the shared human endeavor with all its contingencies and perils. And while his writing charted the costs and metaphysical isolation these individuals often endured, it also emphasized their ability to adapt and to maintain a sense of identity and agency.

Some even find that their conditions spur them to startling creative achievement. A young woman with a low IQ learns to sing arias in more than thirty languages. Another woman finds, at the age of ninety or so, that her forgotten childhood has been restored to her by a bout of involuntary nostalgia, which causes songs from her youth to magically replay themselves in her brain.

In writing about these people, Sacks illuminated the complexities of the human mind and argued for a new, more humane medicine that might integrate matters of physiology and psychology with those of the imagination and the soul. In his own writing, to use the words he once employed to describe the work of the great medical writer A. R. Luria, "Science became poetry, and the pathos of radical lostness was evoked."

WHERE THE WILD THINGS ARE

(1963)

Story and Pictures by Maurice Sendak

C hildren surviving childhood," Maurice Sendak once said in an interview, "is my obsessive theme and my life's concern." His books like *Outside Over There, In the Night Kitchen,* and his enduring masterpiece, *Where the Wild Things Are,* are all testaments to Sendak's understanding that children are "small, courageous people who have to deal every day with a multitude of problems, just as we do"; they are "unprepared for most things, and what they most yearn for is a bit of truth somewhere."

His books served up those truths with uncommon inventiveness, honesty, and humor, capturing both the pleasures of childhood and children's untamed capacity for wonder, and its dark side—fears of abandonment and loss, a sense of vulnerability in a chaotic world where control and understanding feel elusive. At the same time, he captured children's resilience—their remarkable resourcefulness and courage and ability to shape their own destiny.

The tale of Max—the mischief-making boy in the white wolf suit, who journeys to the land where the wild things dwell—embodies all these perennial Sendak themes. The book's captivating and now iconic drawings depict children's ability to traverse the realms of reality and fantasy with magical ease, while the story chronicles how a young boy—who has been sent to his room without dinner, for acting like a wild thing—uses fantasy to confront and master the frightening emotions of anger and frustration. He conjures a little boat that transports him, through night and day, to "the place where the wild things are," roaring their terrible roars and gnashing their terrible teeth. Max tames these wild beasts—and his own emotions—with authority and flair, and the wild things crown him "the most wild thing of all."

As their new king, Max declares, "Let the wild rumpus start!" and in a series of three glorious double-spread layouts, Sendak gives us singular images of the celebratory festivities that ensue—images so kinetic, so vibrant, we can almost hear the music playing as Max and the monsters gambol under the pale moonlight. And then Max sends the wild things off to bed—the same way his mother sent him off to bed, without his supper. Feeling lonely, he heads home, sailing back across the world, to his bedroom, where "he found his supper waiting for him"—"and it was still hot."

Max's use of his imagination—to both liberate himself and tame his emotions—echoes Sendak's own discovery, when he was a sickly young boy who was often confined to bed, that imagination was a gift that enabled him to transform his own fears into beautiful and indelible art.

BOOKS BY DR. SEUSS

HORTON HEARS A WHO! (1954)

THE CAT IN THE HAT (1957)

HOW THE GRINCH STOLE CHRISTMAS! (1957)

GREEN EGGS AND HAM (1960)

THE LORAX (1971)

OH, THE PLACES YOU'LL GO! (1990)

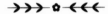

What was the name of your first book?
The book that taught you how to read,
And made you love words on a page,
The book that made reading a need.

For me, it was Seuss—Dr., that is,
Who could write and draw with equal style,
Who created animals both zany and real,
Who taught us how to read with a smile.

In Seussland we were lucky to meet
The feathered and fuzzy and furry.
Beasties dressed in hats, mittens, and socks,
Creatures who always seemed in a hurry.

In book after book, they twitter and woof,
They yitter and yap, and the humming fish hum.
His creatures are shaggy and splendid and squishy.
They persevere, whatever may come.

We're sick of old Dick and sick of old Jane,
Sick of their stupid dog Spot.
It's Dr. Seuss who made reading fun,
Who taught what could never be taught.

Yes, yes, it's truer than true:
The great doctor made fun that was funny!
A world with Grinches and Sneetches,
Where the weather was wicked and sunny.

Seuss was able to make language dance
With a very American cool.
He conjured old realms like Mulberry Street,
And new ones like the Jungle of Nool.

There was a Nook, a Zans, a Gox, and a Ying,
A cat in a hat, and a fox in blue socks,
A Lorax who speaks for the trees,
And Thing 1 and Thing 2, who live in a box.

He captured the "howling mad hullabaloo"
Out there in the world that sprang from his head.
With ink in his pen and rhymes in his brain,
He took us past Zebra, and way beyond zed.

What was the name of your first book?
The book that taught you how to read,
And made you love words on a page.
A Seuss book, most of us agreed!

THE PLAYS OF
WILLIAM SHAKESPEARE

>>> ❖ <<<

Four centuries after his death, Shakespeare remains the most contemporary of writers—performed around the world in myriad languages and across disparate cultures. He has shaped the writing and the imaginations of writers and thinkers, from Dostoyevsky and Melville, to President Lincoln and President Obama, to Kierkegaard, Nietzsche, Freud, Baudelaire, Brecht, and Beckett. And become part of the very literary air we breathe. The structure of Hollywood's romantic comedies, the use of stream-of-consciousness asides in novels and television shows, even turns of phrase that have entered the language (like "brave new world," and the "sound and fury"), can all be traced back to Shakespeare. As a character in Jane Austen's *Mansfield Park* put it, "one gets acquainted" with his work "without knowing how."

Whenever I am asked what I would choose as my "desert island" book—the one book I would choose to have with me if I were shipwrecked on a remote island—I always say Shakespeare's plays: they are endlessly fascinating, so layered and complex, so staggering in simple terms of language, that you could read and reread them, again and again, until a rescue boat arrived (or didn't arrive). His plays remind us of the miracle of the human imagination, which defies the most basic laws of physics—the creation of something from nothing (or nearly nothing—some shards of old recycled plotlines), and the invention of teeming, populous worlds, now known to schoolchildren across the globe.

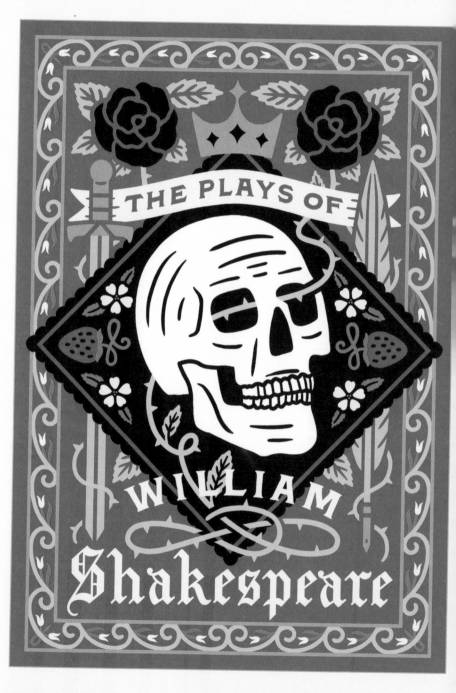

THE PLAYS OF

WILLIAM

Shakespeare

Shakespeare's plays define such fundamental aspects of the human condition that one generation after another has claimed him as their own, filtering his work through prisms that reflect readers' own social, political, and cultural concerns. Many Restoration critics saw Shakespeare as a public dramatic poet addressing issues of the day, while the Romantics stressed his role as a writer who understood the joys and disappointments of love. In recent years, scholars have commented on the modernity of Shakespeare's techniques—mixing and remaking genres, fusing highbrow art and popular entertainment, breaking the fourth wall of the stage—even as audiences marvel at the contemporaneity of his spirited, independent heroines and his self-dramatizing characters so preoccupied with questions of identity and plural truths.

One of the reasons for Shakespeare's perennial appeal lies in the fact that his plays are completed—and continually reinvented—by actors who bring their own experiences to a production. As Nicholas Hytner, the former artistic director of London's National Theatre and renowned Shakespeare director, observed in a 2013 lecture, "the real Shakespeare" was "an actor who provides for other actors an infinite, myriad of ways of telling his stories and of being his characters," and his plays, like a musical score, "need players to become music."

As for the world of change and loss depicted in Shakespeare's plays, it feels uncannily familiar to contemporary readers, too. His political plays (most notably *Richard III, Julius Caesar, Macbeth,* and *Coriolanus*) examine the dynamics of tyranny and political perfidy with an acuity that resonates today, when autocracy is on the rise around the world and democracy is increasingly in retreat.

In his influential 1964 book, *Shakespeare, Our Contemporary,* the Polish critic Jan Kott looked at his plays as mirrors that could reflect back the history of our own times. Kott also examined the affinities between Shakespeare and such avatars of the theater of the absurd as Beckett, Ionesco, and Genet, arguing that plays like *Hamlet* and *King Lear* evinced a dark, uncompromising, and very modern view of the world as an irrational place, ruled by violence and chance, a place where "it is the clowns who tell the truth."

The Elizabethan era, like our own, was grappling with the unsettling fallout of rapid progress and globalization. Thanks to the printing press, literacy was spreading, and traditional divisions between the classes were dissolving. Explorers were opening up the world, and astronomers were on the verge of discoveries that would shatter people's sense of cosmic order.

It was, as Kott wrote, an era of science and innovation and "the most magnificent architectural exploits," but also an age of religious wars, toxic political strife, city-decimating plagues, and growing uncertainty and disillusion. An age that forced people to grapple with "the divergence between dreams and reality; between human potentialities and the misery of one's lot"—and in that respect, an age not unlike our own.

FRANKENSTEIN

(1818)

Mary Shelley
Edited by David H. Guston, Ed Finn, and Jason Scott Robert
(MIT Press, 2017)

→→→ ✿ ←←←

Two centuries after it was published, Mary Shelley's *Frankenstein* is acknowledged as one of the foundation stones of science fiction and modern horror. It's inspired countless contemporary tales about scientific hubris and technology run amok like the *Jurassic Park* and *Terminator* franchises. It's been read as a parable about the dangers of men trying to usurp the powers of God or appropriate the procreative power of women, and as an allegory about Western imperialism and the terrible human costs of colonialism and slavery.

The novel—which Shelley started when she was eighteen—is ingeniously constructed as a series of stories within stories, and it stands, like Emily Brontë's *Wuthering Heights,* as one of the most innovative works in nineteenth-century English literature.

As biographers have pointed out, the themes of *Frankenstein* were actually deeply rooted in Mary Shelley's own life, from her exposure, as the daughter of Mary Wollstonecraft and William Godwin, to radical political and philosophical ideas, to her own haunting association of birth and death, because of a series of personal tragedies (her mother died from postpartum complications, less than two weeks after her birth; her first child with Shelley died after living only twelve days). Even the creature's sense of rejection, when Victor

Frankenstein summarily abandons him, would have been familiar to the teenage Mary, who was scorned for eloping with the married Percy and denounced by her own father.

Unlike many movie versions, Mary Shelley's novel makes it clear that it's Victor who's the real monster, not the creature he has brought to life. Shelley is not assailing all science here, so much as the heedless pursuit of scientific innovation without regard to consequences. Victor is guilty of unaccommodated ambition and pride. And Victor is also guilty of being a negligent parent who lacks empathy for the creature he brought into the world and who leaves him to a miserable, solitary existence—lonely, spurned by everyone he meets, and forced to educate himself (movie adaptations tend to leave out the touching scenes in which the creature learns about human beings and good and evil by reading *Paradise Lost, The Sorrows of Young Werther,* and *Plutarch's Lives*).

Victor Frankenstein's neglect of the creature he has brought into the world is the focus of a 2017 edition of the novel published by the MIT Press and "annotated for scientists, engineers, and creators of all kinds." The novel, the book's editors write, "prompts serious reflection about our individual and collective responsibility for nurturing the products of our creativity and imposing constraints on our capacities to change the world around us"—a particularly important concept "in an era of synthetic biology, genome editing, robotics, machine learning, and regenerative medicine."

One endnote in the MIT edition notes that the remorse Victor feels after his despondent creature begins killing people is "reminiscent of J. Robert Oppenheimer's sentiments when he witnessed the unspeakable power of the atomic bomb" and famously remarked, "I am become death, the destroyer of worlds."

LITTLE FAILURE

(2014)

Gary Shteyngart

Gary Shteyngart's *Little Failure* is the funniest memoir I've read. It's also a moving, tender, irreverent, earnest, and keenly observed account of what it's like to grow up as an immigrant in 1980s New York—an account that testifies to the author's exuberant gift for storytelling and his jet-fueled love of language.

Shteyngart was seven when his parents packed all their possessions into two green sacks and three orange suitcases and moved the family from Leningrad to Queens, New York. And like his delightful novels *Super Sad True Love Story* and *The Russian Debutante's Handbook,* this memoir showcases his high-frequency radar for the absurdities of life in both the monochromatic world of the Soviet Union and the perplexing and gloriously Technicolor world of the United States.

In *Little Failure,* Shteyngart gives us a hilarious account of his own clumsy efforts to adapt to life in the country he'd learned, as a child, to regard as "the enemy." At the same time, he poignantly conveys his parents' hard-fought efforts to make new lives for themselves in America and the simultaneous love and exasperation he feels for them as he embarks on his own American dream of becoming a writer.

Along the way, Shteyngart makes us understand the strict ground rules of his parents' frugal, cautious existence in the States.

On a car trip, they take their own food (soft-boiled eggs wrapped in tinfoil, Russian beet salad, cold chicken) into a McDonald's. They help themselves to the free napkins and straws while spurning the sixty-nine-cent hamburgers as an unnecessary extravagance.

After considerable family discussion, the author's birth name, Igor, is changed to Gary, because "Igor is Frankenstein's assistant, and I have enough problems already," and because Gary summons pleasant associations with the actor Gary Cooper. The new name, however, doesn't help much when it comes to learning classmates' cultural vocabulary. Without a television set at home, Gary spends his free time reading Chekhov stories but quickly learns that "these little porkers" at school "have very little interest in 'Gooseberries' or 'Lady with Lapdog.'"

The title of his memoir, Shteyngart explains, came from a nickname his mother gave him, "*Failurchka,* or Little Failure." Little Failure because his grades at Stuyvesant High School weren't good enough to get him into an Ivy League college, which means, his parents suggest, they "may as well have never come here." Little Failure because a career as a writer isn't quite the vocation his parents had envisioned: "Everyone knows that immigrant children have to go into law, medicine, or maybe that strange new category known only as 'computer.'"

Back in the U.S.S.R., Gary had begun writing his first novel— a patriotic tale called "Lenin and His Magical Goose"—when he was an asthmatic five-year-old eager to please his grandmother. For every page he wrote, his grandmother gave him a slice of cheese, and for every completed chapter, a sandwich with bread, butter, and cheese.

"I am saying, *Grandmother: Please love me.* It's a message, both desperate and common, that I will extend to her and to my parents and, later, to a bunch of yeshiva schoolchildren in Queens and, still later, to my several readers around the world."

WHITE TEETH

(2000)

Zadie Smith

White Teeth, Zadie Smith's spectacular debut novel published when she was twenty-four years old, is a big, splashy, populous production with the humane, comic vitality of Charles Dickens; a fascination with the themes of exile and migration shared with Salman Rushdie; and the ambition and verbal energy of David Foster Wallace. Smith possesses both an instinctive storytelling talent and a thoroughly original voice that's street-smart and learned, audacious and philosophical all at the same time.

On the surface, *White Teeth* recounts the misadventures of two World War II veterans—Archie Jones, an unassuming Englishman, and his best friend, Samad Iqbal, a Bengali Muslim—and the stories of their extended and very dysfunctional families. Smith writes with magical access to her characters' inner lives, delineating their romantic and familial travails with empathy and humor while at the same time opening out her story to look at the broader cultural and political dynamics that inform their daily lives. Her novel is a story about parents and children, friends and neighbors, and a larger story about immigration and exile and the legacy of British colonialism.

White Teeth takes place in a cacophonous London of curry shops and pool halls and cheap hair salons—a city peopled by "Becks, B-boys, Indie kids, wide-boys, ravers, rudeboys, Acidheads, Sharons, Tracies, Kevs, Nation Brothers, Raggas, and Pakis"; a city where frustrated waiters dream of changing history and the once unforgiving lines of race and class have blurred.

Smith's characters cope with the social flux around them in very different ways. Her hero Archie, who is married to a young Jamaican woman named Clara, deals with all the change and chaos with good-natured humor. He wonders why people can't "just get on with things, just live together, you know, in peace or harmony or something." His best friend, Samad, in contrast, rages against the decadence of contemporary culture and the corrupting effect he sees it having on his twin teenage sons.

For Smith, Archie and Samad are representatives of two worldviews: one practical-minded and pragmatic, the other ideological and absolutist; one accepting of randomness as a by-product of freedom, the other determined to try to stage-manage fate. Archie, who works for a direct-mail company, designing folds for its folders, accepts the fact that he is "a man whose significance in the Greater Scheme of Things could be figured along familiar ratios" of pebble to beach, raindrop to ocean, needle to haystack; he is happy to go with the flow. Samad, on his part, remains obsessed with the role his great-grandfather played in the Indian mutiny; he craves glory and distinction and rages against his own lowly job as a waiter.

Samad sends Magid, the more accommodating of his twin sons, back home to Bangladesh to receive a proper Muslim education. That way, he figures, at least one of his boys will grow up proud of his familial and cultural roots. His blueprint for his boys' future does not exactly work out as planned. Magid returns home from Bangladesh an ardent Anglophile, a would-be lawyer who wears white suits and talks like David Niven. His brother, Millat, meanwhile, joins a radical Islamic group that preaches revolution and renunciation.

In recounting a series of increasingly antic events that overtake Archie's and Samad's families, Smith gently sends up her characters' vanities and self-delusions while showing how one generation often revolts against another—sons against fathers, daughters against mothers—but also how they repeat their predecessors' mistakes, retrace their ancestors' dreams, and how, as immigrants and their children, they struggle to embrace their sense of doubleness and dual inheritances.

With this extraordinarily precocious debut, Smith announced herself as a novelist of remarkable powers, a writer with talents commensurate with her ambitions.

MY BELOVED WORLD

(2013)

Sonia Sotomayor

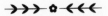

When she was starting out in the Manhattan district attorney's office in the early 1980s, Sonia Sotomayor—who was named to the Supreme Court by President Obama in 2009—was taught by one of her bosses that as a prosecutor she could not appeal to logic alone, but needed to use emotion to make jurors feel the "moral responsibility to convict." The state's case "is a narrative: the story of a crime," she wrote in her 2013 memoir, *My Beloved World*. "It is the particulars that make a story real. In examining witnesses, I learned to ask general questions so as to elicit details with powerful sensory associations: the colors, the sounds, the smells that lodge an image in the mind and put the listener in the burning house."

It's a searching and powerfully observed memoir about identity and coming of age, about the American dream realized through extraordinary will and dedication.

My Beloved World attests to just how adeptly Justice Sotomayor mastered the art of narrative. It's a searching and powerfully observed memoir about identity and coming of age, about the American dream realized through extraordinary will and dedication. Writing in evocative, plainspoken prose, Justice Sotomayor provides an earnest, soul-searching look back at her childhood as the daughter of Puerto Rican parents in New York City and at her education and years as a lawyer. She provides a visceral sense of what it was like to grow up in the Bronx in the 1960s and 1970s, in a neighborhood where stairwells were to be avoided (because of muggers and addicts shooting up) and where tourniquets and glassine packets littered the sidewalks.

Young Sotomayor was sustained by a sense of discipline, perseverance, and stoic self-reliance developed from learning how to manage her diabetes (she started giving herself insulin shots at seven because her parents seemed unable to deal with the procedure) and from her awareness, as a child, of the uncertainties of daily life, slammed home by her father's drinking and her mother's angry response to his alcoholism (which took the form of working nights and weekends to avoid being at home).

It was the love and protection of her grandmother Abuelita, Justice Sotomayor writes, that gave her "a refuge from the chaos at home" and allowed her "to imagine the most improbable of possibilities for my life."

As a girl, Sonia became fascinated with the idea of becoming a lawyer or judge from watching *Perry Mason*. Her first dream, however, was of becoming a detective like her favorite heroine, Nancy Drew. Her mind worked in similar ways to Nancy's, she told herself: "I was a keen observer and listener. I picked up on clues. I figured things out logically, and I enjoyed puzzles. I loved the clear, focused feeling that came when I concentrated on solving a problem and everything else faded out."

Justice Sotomayor writes as someone with considerable self-knowledge, and she points out that there has been a recurrent pattern in her life. Whether it was Princeton, Yale Law School, the Manhattan DA's office, or an appointment to the bench, the challenges of a new environment would initially lead to a period "of fevered insecurity, a reflexive terror that I'll fall flat on my face," followed by "ferocious compensatory effort." She had learned from her mother, she says, that "a surplus of effort could overcome a deficit of confidence."

In college she received a C on her first midterm paper and realized she needed to learn how to construct more coherent arguments and that she also needed to improve her English. Over the next few summers, she says, she devoted each day's lunch hour to grammar exercises and to learning ten new words, and to catching up on classics—like *Adventures of Huckleberry Finn* and *Pride and Prejudice*—that she had missed out on reading as a child.

Fear of leaving anything to chance—another legacy of her unstable childhood—made her prepare intensively for classwork and legal cases. And her single-minded devotion to work paid off. Just as she became adept at collecting gold stars as a schoolgirl, so she graduated from Princeton summa cum laude and, as a prosecutor, began racking up convictions. Her first day in open court as a new federal judge in 1992 made her so nervous she felt her knees were literally knocking together, but she soon realized that she had found her vocation.

"I think," she wrote, "this fish has found her pond."

THE PALM AT THE END
OF THE MIND

Selected Poems and a Play

(1971)

Wallace Stevens
Edited by Holly Stevens

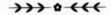

Ο ne of my favorite stories about the writing habits of well-known authors concerns Wallace Stevens.

Stevens worked for almost four decades at the Hartford Accident and Indemnity Company, where he became a vice president, and every weekday he would walk the two miles from his home in a pleasant residential neighborhood of Hartford to his downtown office. While he was walking, he composed, in his head, the shimmering, musical verse that would earn him recognition as one of America's preeminent poets. By one account, he liked to time words to the rhythm of his steps, pausing or taking a step back when he was stuck on a rhyme or a line. According to his daughter, Holly, he might jot down the occasional note, but he worked the verses out in his head, then dictated the completed poems to his secretary at the office.

Stevens, who wore gray suits seven days a week, was known in the insurance world as the "dean of surety claims men," but in his poems he assumed a succession of antic personae: clowns, dandies, and fops, characters like Peter Quince and Crispin the Comedian.

Stevens's backyard garden and Hartford's Elizabeth Park, where he took his daughter to feed the ducks, helped inspire some of the

WALLACE

STEVENS

THE
PALM
AT
THE
END
OF
THE
MIND

lovely images of nature in his poems—nature, whose seasonal cycles tended to trigger in him both dizzying despair at the thought of things continually changing and repeating themselves, and hope in the ongoing renewal of life.

In many of his most celebrated poems, Stevens returns again and again to the relationship between reality and the human imagination, between the world as it is and the world as it is transformed by perception and art. "I placed a jar in Tennessee," he wrote in one of his best-known poems, "And round it was, upon a hill. / It made the slovenly wilderness / Surround that hill."

And in "The Idea of Order at Key West": "It was her voice that made / The sky acutest at its vanishing. / She measured to the hour its solitude. / She was the single artificer of the world / In which she sang. And when she sang, the sea, / Whatever self it had, became the self / That was her song, for she was the maker."

As Stevens's biographer Joan Richardson has observed, Stevens's double life as a poet and an insurance executive enabled him to fulfill both his own youthful dreams of literary success and his father's puritanical expectations. This double life allowed him to live part time in an abstract realm of his own making, part time in the hard-nosed business world of facts. Indeed, the process by which his imagination created "rubbings against reality" not only gave birth to individual poems but also became the central theme of his work.

Stevens had always nursed a horror of disorder, carefully organizing his day-to-day life around his office routines, and he slowly learned to use his imagination as a tool for subduing the chaos around him. Eventually, Richardson wrote, "he was able to transform the desire for God, learned from his mother, into a desacramentalized version: the 'delight in the harmonious and orderly.'"

Poetry, "the supreme fiction," had become, for him, a substitute for religion—and, in his words, a "completion of life."

THE GOLDFINCH

(2013)

Donna Tartt

I t's impossible to read Donna Tartt's glorious 2013 novel, *The Goldfinch,* and not think of the work of Charles Dickens. Although the book's title comes from a charming seventeenth-century painting of a bird by the Dutch artist Carel Fabritius, its characters and melodramatic plot are clearly the work of an author who has inhaled and absorbed the novels of Charles Dickens and magically exhaled them into a fully imagined, post-9/11 novel that is an enthralling testament to her own storytelling gifts.

It's a book that shows us Tartt's growth and reach as a novelist. The central themes of *The Goldfinch*—loss and death and the fragility of ordinary life—are ones she's dealt with before. But in these pages, she's fused together the suspense of her gripping debut novel, *The Secret History* (1992), with the ability, developed in her 2002 novel, *The Little Friend,* to map her characters' inner lives with exceptional emotional exactitude. In fact, *The Goldfinch* points to Tartt's range as a writer, capable of grappling with the sorts of big philosophical questions addressed by the great nineteenth-century novelists and the more interior struggles mapped by many contemporary authors. At the same time, she uses her instinctive sense of mood and place to give us a digital-sharp portrait of America in the twenty-first century. She captures the enduring social rituals of Manhattan's Upper East Side, the small-town rhythms of Greenwich Village, and the "hot mineral emptiness" of a Las Vegas desert neighborhood, full of empty houses in foreclosure.

Like *Great Expectations*, *The Goldfinch* concerns the moral and sentimental education of an orphan and a mysterious benefactor. The story begins with an event that splits thirteen-year-old Theo Decker's life into a Before and After: he and his mother stop by the Metropolitan Museum of Art, where one of her favorite paintings—Fabritius's *Goldfinch*—is on exhibit, when a terrorist bomb suddenly explodes. Theo's mother is killed in the explosion, and in the chaotic aftermath he impulsively grabs *The Goldfinch* from the burning wreckage. The painting comes to be a sort of talisman of his mother's love, and his reluctance to return it to the museum will propel him into a series of increasingly dangerous adventures, involving drug dealers, art thieves, and mobsters.

His companion on these adventures is his new friend Boris, a funny, profane, street-smart kid who grew up in Australia, Russia, and Ukraine and who plays Artful Dodger to Theo's Oliver Twist. The irrepressible Boris is one of those memorable characters—so kinetic, so uninhibited, so utterly real—who will take up permanent residence in our minds.

Some of the plot developments in *The Goldfinch* may sound ridiculously contrived in summary. But Tartt uses coincidence and improbable events, much the way Dickens did, to leave readers with a deeply felt appreciation of the randomness of life and fate's sometimes cruel sense of humor, as well as the very American belief in fresh starts and second acts.

DEMOCRACY IN AMERICA

VOLUME 1 (1835)

VOLUME 2 (1840)

Alexis de Tocqueville
Translated by Henry Reeve

I n 1831, a twenty-five-year-old French aristocrat named Alexis
de Tocqueville and his friend Gustave de Beaumont set sail
for America to see the fledgling democracy that had captured
their imagination. Their nine-month road trip would result in
Tocqueville's classic study, *Democracy in America*—a book that
combined its young author's keen reportorial eye with his analytic
skills as a social historian.

Tocqueville—two of whose grandparents were killed in the
Terror following the French Revolution—worried that democracies
could devolve into a new kind of tyranny, but he also embraced
democracy and egalitarianism as the wave of the future. He and
Beaumont traveled by horseback, canoe, and steamboat through
seventeen states, interviewing a wide array of Americans, and from
his copious notes Tocqueville wrote a remarkably clear-eyed book
that was clairvoyant in its diagnosis of the American psyche and
the possibilities—and dangers—inherent in democracy as a form
of governance.

Writing a century and a half before social media accelerated the
sorting of people into silos of like-minded souls, Tocqueville noted

Americans' tendency to withdraw into "small, private circles, united together by the similitude of their conditions, habits, and manners," in order "to indulge by themselves in the enjoyments of private life." He worried that this self-absorption would diminish a sense of duty to the larger community, opening the way for a kind of soft tyranny that "compresses, enervates, extinguishes, and stupefies a people." This was one possible cost of a society preoccupied with materialistic success, he predicted, where people become so focused on procuring "the petty and paltry pleasures with which they glut their lives" that they neglect their responsibilities as citizens. It was difficult to imagine, he wrote, how people who "have entirely given up the habit of self-government should succeed in making a proper choice of those by whom they are to be governed."

Tocqueville was concerned that anti-elitism, combined with a disinclination to carefully study a candidate's qualifications, could make a democracy susceptible to "mountebanks of all sorts" who clamor to tell the crowd what it wants to hear. The dangers of populism, he suggested, could be seen in President Andrew Jackson, whom he described as "a man of violent temper and very moderate talents," opposed by "the majority of the enlightened classes of the Union"—a man who "tramples on his personal enemies, whenever

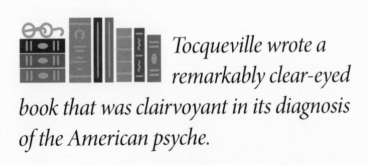 *Tocqueville wrote a remarkably clear-eyed book that was clairvoyant in its diagnosis of the American psyche.*

they cross his path," even treating members of Congress "with disdain approaching to insult." Jackson's conduct as president of the federal government, Tocqueville wrote, "may be reckoned as one of the dangers that threaten its continuance."

Tocqueville's harshest words were aimed at the two original sins committed by Americans on the continent: "the rapacity of the settlers," backed by "the tyranny of the government," which led to the removal and extermination of Native American tribes; and slavery, which resulted in "such unparalleled atrocities as suffice to show that the laws of humanity have been totally perverted." Tocqueville predicted that slavery could lead "to the most horrible of civil wars."

Among the myriad other predictions in *Democracy in America*—many of them uncannily foresighted—is that in the years to come, two nations seem "marked out by the will of Heaven to sway the destinies of half the globe": America, giving "free scope to the unguided strength and common sense of the people"; and Russia, centering all "authority of society" on its ruler. "The principal instrument of the former is freedom; of the latter, servitude."

THE LORD OF THE RINGS

THE FELLOWSHIP OF THE RING (1954)

THE TWO TOWERS (1954)

THE RETURN OF THE KING (1955)

J. R. R. Tolkien

When I visualize Tolkien's *Lord of the Rings*, I don't think of Peter Jackson's movies; I think of the 1965 Ballantine boxed set of books, with Barbara Remington's charming folk-art covers: a blossoming tree symbolizing the Arcadian paradise of the Shire (*The Fellowship of the Ring*), a mountainous landscape featuring a horde of evil black creatures flying across the sky (*The Two Towers*), and the menacing Mount Doom, erupting in fire as frightening creatures roam the valleys below (*The Return of the King*).

I don't remember exactly how word of mouth worked back in those pre-internet days, but in the late 1960s the Tolkien novels seemed to be what the cool kids at school and their older brothers and sisters were reading. Back then, *The Lord of the Rings* was what the *Harry Potter* novels would become decades later. Kids named their pets Frodo and Gandalf and debated (in what we thought were heavy, intellectual conversations) whether Sauron was a stand-in for Hitler or whether the destructive power of the ring was a metaphor for the atomic bomb.

As kids, we were mesmerized by the cosmic showdown between good and evil, and we also loved that the hero of the story wasn't a knight in shining armor or one of those chiseled warriors pictured on Greek vases but a short, kindhearted orphan from a small town. We didn't know that Tolkien was an authority on Middle English and Anglo-Saxon or that *The Lord of the Rings* drew upon the Grail legend, *Beowulf,* and Tolkien's own experiences as a soldier during World War I. And we didn't know that the story was a nearly perfect paradigm of the mythic template that Joseph Campbell called the "hero's journey."

Two things about *The Lord of the Rings* stood out to me, at the time. The first was just how fully imagined Middle-earth was: Tolkien had conjured a world, complete with its own history, geography, languages, and cultures—a place that was incredibly tangible to me. In fact, I avoided seeing any of the movie adaptations of *The Lord of the Rings* because I didn't want cinematic images crowding out the vivid, minutely detailed maps of Middle-earth that Tolkien's words had inscribed in my head.

The second reason I was so moved by *The Lord of the Rings* had to do with its ending. Yes, the ring is destroyed, Sauron is defeated, and peace is restored to the Shire, but there is no guarantee that dark times—the "Great Danger"—won't one day return to Middle-earth. And Frodo can't simply settle back into his old life in the Shire: he has been changed by his long journey. Weary and still suffering from the wounds he has sustained, he leaves the Shire at the end of the story, traveling with Bilbo, Gandalf, and many of the elves to the Undying Lands in the West. It was 1968—a year when many of us first became aware of the terrible things happening in the world that couldn't be undone—and the ending of *The Lord of the Rings* felt more real and true to me, even at thirteen, than the conventional happy endings of so many other books I'd read up till then.

The Letters of

VINCENT
VAN GOGH

THE LETTERS OF VINCENT
VAN GOGH

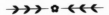

His paintings are instantly recognizable: the incandescent sun-filled canvases from his days in the South of France, phosphorescent stars cartwheeling through a nighttime sky, a clutch of radiant irises lighting up a garden, a flock of crows winging their way across a golden expanse of wheat fields under a stormy sky.

In fact, the words used to describe the French painter Eugène Delacroix and memorized by Vincent van Gogh apply perfectly to van Gogh himself: he had "a sun in his head and a thunderstorm in his heart."

An ardent lover of books, van Gogh was a gifted writer who chronicled his creative process—and in some cases, the genesis of particular paintings—in hundreds of letters, including more than six hundred and fifty to his brother Theo, who was often his one source of creative, emotional, and financial support.

These letters read like a journal—unedited, almost stream-of-consciousness outpourings of what Vincent was painting, drawing, reading, seeing, thinking. There is enormous immediacy to his writing as he chronicles his loneliness, depression, and restless search for meaning. "There may be a great fire in your soul," he writes in 1880, "but no one ever comes to warm himself by it, all that passers-by can see is a little smoke coming out of the chimney and they walk on."

Van Gogh had turned to drawing after a failed effort to become a pastor like his father. Art, he realized, helped fill the spiritual hole in his heart, and his letters form an extraordinary account of his dedication to his newfound vocation and his iron-willed determination to learn how to paint. He struggled on in the face of disapproval from his family, disparaging remarks from early teachers, and discouraging sales.

In his letters, he writes about the artists he learned from (Rembrandt, Millet, the pointillists, and Japanese printmakers) and the writers he admired (like Shakespeare, Zola, Dickens, George Eliot). He writes about his thoughts on color and light, his experimentation with new techniques, his frustrations with his craft. "I long so much to make beautiful things," he wrote to Theo in 1882. "But beautiful things require effort—and disappointment and perseverance."

Reading these letters, we understand how van Gogh willed himself to become a painter, ceaselessly studying other artists, and how he assimilated and transformed those lessons from the museum in his head into his own transcendent and transformative art.

The letters—which contain sketches of some of his most famous paintings—are an essential companion to his electric art. "I have a certain obligation and duty," he wrote to Theo in 1883, "because I've walked the earth for thirty years," to leave a "certain souvenir in the form of drawings or paintings in gratitude."

ON EARTH WE'RE BRIEFLY GORGEOUS

(2019)

Ocean Vuong

In his stunning 2016 poetry collection, *Night Sky with Exit Wounds,* Ocean Vuong—who was born on a rice farm outside Saigon in 1988 and arrived in the United States at the age of two—used the magic of words to conjure and preserve the memories of family members, to turn "bones to sonatas," and, by pressing pen to paper, to touch them "back from extinction."

Vuong was raised by his grandmother and mother—neither of whom could read—in Hartford, Connecticut, where his mother worked in a nail salon to support the family. Because his grandmother had married an American serviceman during the Vietnam War, he observed in one of his poems, an irony of that war was this: "no bombs—no family—no me."

Many of Vuong's poems focused on Vietnam and his family's efforts to grapple with memories of the war. His lyrical debut novel, *On Earth We're Briefly Gorgeous,* also looks at the emotional fallout of Vietnam. It is also an unsparing rumination on identity—on what it means to be an immigrant, a gay man, a writer who first learned to cherish language because his mother and grandmother needed him to be their interpreter. He describes growing up poor in Hartford— bicycling an hour to a summer job that paid nine dollars an hour, looking for items at Goodwill with a yellow tag (because that meant an extra 50 percent off), and eating sandwiches made with Wonder Bread and mayonnaise (which his mother thought was butter) and "thinking this was the American Dream."

By turns bold and poetic, urgent and elegiac, Vuong's cubist narrative jumps back and forth in time, giving us snapshots from the lives of the narrator and his family. Inspired in part by Vuong's own life, *On Earth We're Briefly Gorgeous* takes the form of a letter from a young man called Little Dog to his illiterate mother. Little Dog tells her about falling in love with a boy named Trevor and the passionate affair they began one summer while working at a local tobacco farm. And he tells her about Trevor dying at the age of twenty-two from an overdose of heroin laced with fentanyl and about four other friends whose lives were claimed by drugs.

We learn that Little Dog's mother suffers from post-traumatic stress disorder—from all the bombings she witnessed during the war, and from the abuse she suffered at the hands of Little Dog's father. We also learn that she often takes out her anger on her son, bullying him, hitting him, throwing things at him. But Little Dog's portrait of his mother is a loving one, filled with shared memories and gratitude for all the sacrifices she and his grandmother made to make his life in America possible.

He remembers her getting dressed up in her best clothes to take him window-shopping at the mall. And he remembers her humming "Happy Birthday" to him when he was young and scared because it was the only song she knew in English.

"When does a war end?" he asks her of her memories of Vietnam. "When can I say your name and have it mean only your name and not what you left behind?"

THE POETRY OF DEREK WALCOTT, 1948-2013

(2014)

Selected by Glyn Maxwell

"I had no nation now but the imagination," Derek Walcott wrote in "The Schooner *Flight*." That line succinctly sums up the themes that animated the Nobel Prize–winning poet's work throughout his career. Born in the West Indies to a family of English, African, and Dutch descent, Walcott grew up a "divided child," caught on the margins of different cultures, and from this mixed inheritance he forged a distinctive poetic voice and a body of work, memorable for its pictorial immediacy, its historical complexity, and its stunning musicality.

In early poems, Walcott wrote of being torn "between the Greek and African pantheon," of having to "choose / Between this Africa and the English tongue I love." His search for an identity is amplified further in the autobiographical poem *Another Life* and in the songs of exile contained in *The Fortunate Traveller*. To be a wanderer between cultures, a prodigal son unable to return home, he implies, is both a blessing and a curse: it means dislocation and cultural disinheritance, but it also means self-reliance and the freedom to invent oneself from "borrowed ancestors."

From what he once called a "sound colonial education," Walcott developed a taste for complicated, formal rhymes, and he absorbed the influence of Shakespeare, Hopkins, and Keats; Homer, Virgil, and Dante. At the same time, his most dynamic verse remains grounded in the particulars of Caribbean history and the heat and light and sound of the sea that he grew up with.

With its innate musicality and dazzling imagery (a reminder that Walcott was also a gifted watercolor painter), his poetry has the power to make readers feel they are seeing things for the first time. In these poems, painterly descriptions of nature (a "moon left on all night among the leaves," leaves on which "the rain splintered like mercury," stars glowing like "fireflies caught in molasses") are combined with literary references and meditations on history and politics to create a compelling myth of the New World: the Antilles, once despoiled by slave traders and imperialism, and now redeemed, re-created anew, like Prospero's secret island, in the poet's imagination.

The "leprosy of empire" has taken its toll in the Caribbean, leaving in its wake terrible poverty and deprivation ("hell is / two hundred shacks on wooden stilts, / one bushy path to the night-soil pits"). But on the islands of the Antilles, there is also the astonishing beauty of a green landscape, illuminated by the radiant light of a southern sky.

Poetry, Walcott said in his 1992 Nobel Lecture, "conjugates both tenses simultaneously: the past and the present." And "the fate of poetry is to fall in love with the world, in spite of History."

INFINITE JEST

(1996)

David Foster Wallace

A prose magician, David Foster Wallace could write about anything and everything with passion and humor and verve—be it tennis or politics or lobsters, the horrors of drug withdrawal or the intricacies of English grammar, the small *ridiculosa* of life aboard a luxury cruise ship or the frightening existential questions humans face when they're not busy trying to distract themselves. He could map the infinite and the infinitesimal, the mythic and the mundane, and fuse the most avant-garde, postmodern pyrotechnics with old-school moral seriousness and introspection.

Infinite Jest gave new meaning to Henry James's description of some novels as "loose baggy monsters." It's a big, psychedelic compendium of strange anecdotes, oddball characters, and self-conscious footnotes, as well as jokes, soliloquies, and digressions that multiply with startling alacrity. The novel not only marked Wallace's embrace of his own exuberant, magpie voice but also challenged all our preconceptions about narrative conventions—about beginnings and endings and closure. In doing so, it became a mirror of the world we were coming to inhabit—a world in which discontinuity is the only constant.

Nearly two and a half decades after it was written, *Infinite Jest* has become one of those landmark books whose influence has

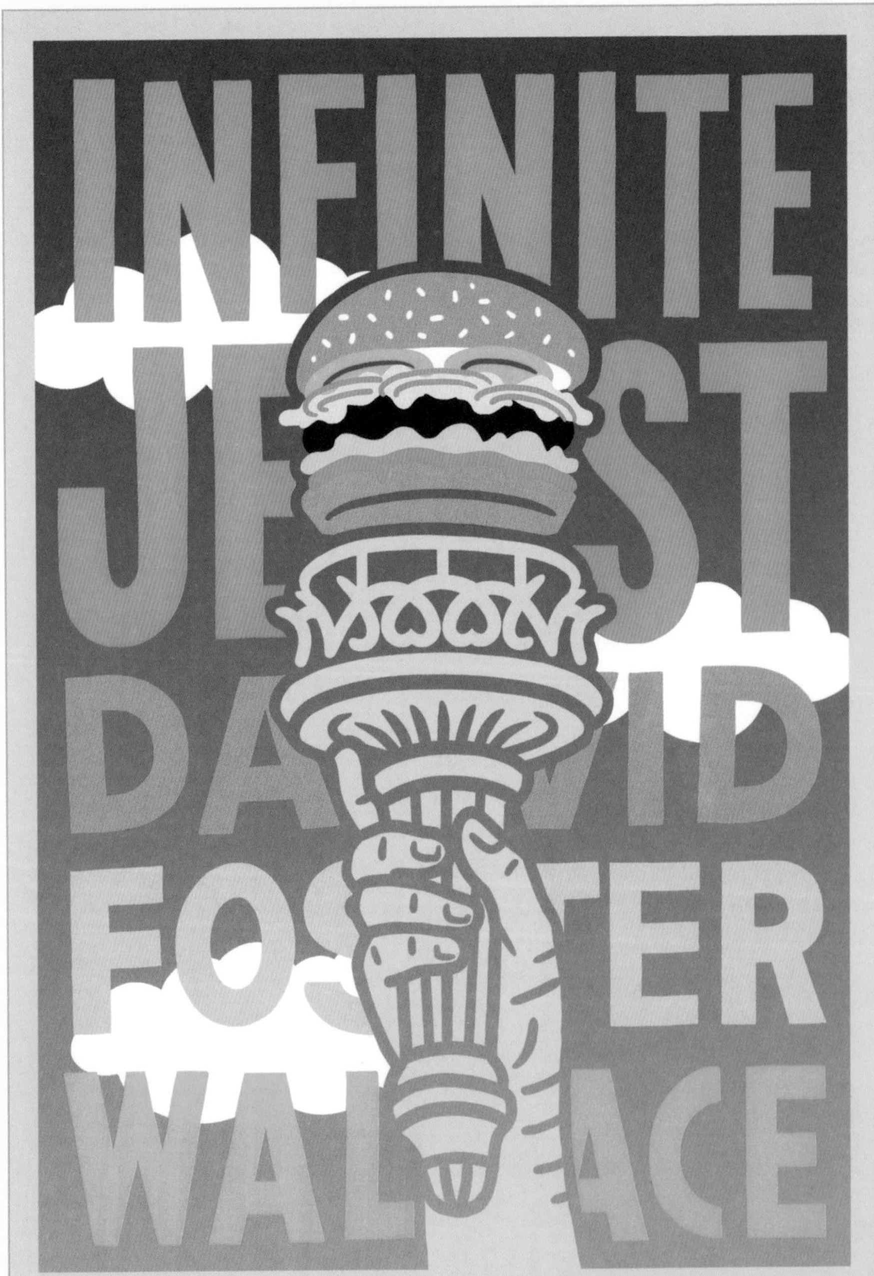
INFINITE
JEST
DAVID
FOSTER
WALLACE

already percolated throughout our culture and whose dystopian vision feels more timely than ever in the twenty-first century.

In its pages, Wallace imagined America's absurd future— in which herds of feral hamsters roam the land—while chronicling the inroads the absurd had already made in a country where advertisements wallpaper our lives and people are overdosing on entertainment, self-gratification, and narcotizing pharmaceuticals. Wallace depicts a country in which each year is named after a particular product (Year of the Trial-Size Dove Bar, Year of the Depend Adult Undergarment, and so on), and the Statue of Liberty serves as a kind of giant billboard, holding aloft huge fake hamburgers and other items in place of her former torch.

As with his posthumously published novel, *The Pale King* (2011), it often feels as though Wallace were deploying every weapon in his astonishing arsenal of talents to capture the cacophony and madness of millennial America: the alienation and loneliness of people living in their self-constructed silos, the daily deluge of data and news and trivia we are pelted with every moment of every day, the relentless commercialization of everything from the landscape to our hobbies and addictions.

He captured what the musician Robert Plant called the myriad "deep and meaningless" facets of life in contemporary America— a place in which reality itself has come to feel surreal.

ALL THE KING'S MEN

(1946)

Robert Penn Warren

The title of *All the King's Men*, Robert Penn Warren's classic parable about power and morality, comes from the nursery rhyme: "Humpty Dumpty sat on a wall, / Humpty Dumpty had a great fall;/ All the king's horses and all the king's men / Couldn't put Humpty together again."

Who is Humpty Dumpty? One answer to this perennial English class question is suggested by Warren's own comments about his original conception of the novel's hero as representing "the kind of doom that democracy may invite upon itself."

Warren's protagonist, Willie Stark, was partly inspired by the life of the Louisiana governor and senator Huey P. Long (1893–1935), whom Mencken described as a "backwoods demagogue" and Hodding Carter II described as "the first true dictator out of the soil of America."

In an essay on the thirty-fifth anniversary of the book, Warren wrote that the first incarnation of Willie was a "political dictator" named Talos in a verse play that he'd worked on during the 1930s. The play was informed by Warren's observations of Huey Long, his teaching of Shakespeare's history plays, his thoughts on Spenser's *Faerie Queene,* and his exposure to the rise of Mussolini while living briefly in Italy. He was interested, Warren wrote, in the theory that "the 'great man' is merely created by historical forces, that he becomes 'great' not from his own isolated strength but from the weakness of others, or from a whole society that has lost its mission."

One character in *All the King's Men* describes Stark as a "hard man": "He's played it hard and close. But there's one principle he's grasped: you don't make omelettes without breaking eggs. And precedents." This was the "alibi of Mussolini and Hitler" and "all grabbers of power," Warren wrote in his 1981 essay, "every Communist and fellow traveler loved to mouth the cliche that you can't make an omelet without breaking eggs. (And that was to be their alibi for Stalin after the Moscow Trials a year or so later.)"

Compared with such notorious tyrants (and even compared with Donald J. Trump), Willie Stark is a complicated character, a politician who began his career with idealistic motives as well as power-hungry ambitions. He rationalizes his chicanery, bullying, and blackmail as means to achieve his goals of helping to improve the lives of the poor and disenfranchised, and learns the dark arts of demagoguery only after he's given this cynical advice: "Hell, make 'em cry, make 'em laugh, make 'em think you're their weak erring pal, or make 'em think you're God-Almighty. Or make 'em mad. Even mad at you. Just stir 'em up, it doesn't matter how or why, and they'll love you and come back for more."

As Warren saw it, Willie Stark possessed "power because he could fulfill some need, some emptiness of those around him." And his story is framed by the story of his political aide Jack Burden, who, in the course of the novel, journeys from alienation and a nihilistic willingness to do anything for "the Boss" to an acceptance of his responsibility for the consequences of his own actions. Jack learns that he cannot sidestep his family's painful past—just as the South cannot avoid coming to terms with the original sin of slavery—and his story underscores the costs of indifference and detachment, and the hazards of believing that one can stand outside history.

EDUCATED

(2018)

Tara Westover

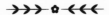

Tara Westover's memoir, *Educated,* is both a moving account of one young woman's remarkable journey of self-discovery and a testament to the power of books and knowledge to transform a life.

Westover, who grew up in the wilds of rural Idaho, the youngest of seven children, never attended school as a child. She learned to read and write by studying the Bible, the Book of Mormon, and speeches by Joseph Smith and Brigham Young.

Her father, a radical survivalist, believed that "public school was a ploy by the Government to lead children away from God"; he stockpiled guns and ammo and canned food supplies and prepared his family for a showdown with the Feds and what he called the "Days of Abomination." He did not believe in doctors or hospitals—even when he and his sons suffered horrifying injuries sustained in car accidents and accidents at his scrap yard. Nor did he or his wife take action when Tara reported that her brother Shawn had been assaulting her.

For years, Tara Westover writes, this was how her life was defined. She was told that as a woman she had no real choices and that her father's word was law. "I knew how my life would play out," she writes, "when I was eighteen or nineteen, I would get married. Dad would give me a corner of the farm, and my husband would put a house on it. Mother would teach me about herbs, and also about midwifery." When she had children of her own, "Mother would deliver them, and one day, I supposed, I would be the Midwife."

Westover recounts the story of her childhood in a direct, matter-of-fact voice. She is equally measured in recounting the extraordinary leap she made from no schooling at all to college and eventually a PhD in history from Cambridge University. Writing this book seems as much a way for her to understand the road she has traveled, as a means of sharing the story of how education completely altered the arc of her life.

That leap began when her older brother Tyler (who had already defied their father and left home for university) encouraged her to study for the ACT college test. Westover drove forty miles to the nearest bookstore to buy a study guide and an algebra textbook, and after months of intensive study she was admitted to Brigham Young University at the age of seventeen. Her father's response: "You have cast aside His blessings to whore after man's knowledge. His wrath is stirred against you. It will not be long in coming."

In college, Westover was startled by the depth of her ignorance: she had never heard of Napoleon or the civil rights movement or the Holocaust. She was aghast at the risqué attire of one of her roommates—Juicy Couture pants and a tank top with spaghetti straps—and startled that fellow students watched movies on Sundays.

But Westover persisted. She won a Gates Scholarship to Cambridge University, became a visiting fellow at Harvard, and returned to Cambridge for her doctorate. The further her studies took her into the world of academia, the further she felt from home. After she told her father about Shawn's threats against her and her sister (and her father cruelly doubled down on Shawn's side), there was finally a break with her parents—a break her father offered to heal, only if she would take back all she had said and done and agree to be "reborn." Though she wanted the love of her parents back, she says she realized that what her father was demanding was nothing less than the surrendering of her "own perceptions of right and wrong, of reality, of sanity itself."

"Everything I had worked for," she writes, "all my years of study, had been to purchase for myself this one privilege: to see and experience more truths than those given to me by my father, and to use those truths to construct my own mind. I had come to believe that the ability to evaluate many ideas, many histories, many points of view, was at the heart of what it means to self-create. If I yielded now, I would lose more than an argument. I would lose custody of my own mind. This was the price I was being asked to pay, I understood that now. What my father wanted to cast from me wasn't a demon: it was me."

"You could call this selfhood many things," she goes on. "Transformation. Metamorphosis. Falsity. Betrayal.

"I call it an education."

THE UNDERGROUND RAILROAD

(2016)

Colson Whitehead

In his harrowing 2016 novel, *The Underground Railroad*, Colson Whitehead turns that covert nineteenth-century network of secret routes and safe houses—run by black and white activists to help slaves escape from the Deep South—into an actual train, a kind of subway running north toward freedom.

The result is a potent, hallucinatory novel that leaves us with a devastating understanding of the terrible human costs of slavery. It's a novel that possesses the chilling, detailed power of the slave narratives collected by the Federal Writers' Project in the 1930s, combined with haunting echoes of Ralph Ellison's *Invisible Man*, Toni Morrison's *Beloved*, and Victor Hugo's *Les Misérables*.

Whitehead's story chronicles the life of a teenage slave named Cora who flees the Georgia plantation where she was born, risking everything in pursuit of freedom, much the way her mother, Mabel, did years before.

Cora and her friend Caesar are pursued by a fanatical, Javert-like slave catcher named Ridgeway whose failure to find Mabel has made him all the more determined to hunt down her daughter and destroy the abolitionist network that has aided her. Traveling from Georgia to South Carolina to North Carolina to Tennessee to Indiana, Cora must try to elude not just Ridgeway but also other bounty hunters, informers, and lynch mobs. She is helped along the way by a few dedicated "railroad" workers who are willing to risk their lives to save hers.

Like his earlier novels *The Intuitionist* and *John Henry Days*, *The Underground Railroad* shows Whitehead's effortless ability to combine unsparing realism with fable-like allegory, the plainspoken with the poetic.

He conveys the emotional fallout of slavery: the fear, the humiliation, the loss of dignity and control. And he conveys the daily brutality of life on the plantation, where Cora is gang-raped, where whippings (accompanied by scrubbings in pepper water to intensify the pain) are routine. Over the years, Whitehead writes, Cora "had seen men hung from trees and left for buzzards and crows. Women carved open to the bones with the cat-o'-nine-tails. Bodies alive and dead roasted on pyres. Feet cut off to prevent escape and hands cut off to stop theft."

In the course of her travels, Cora learns that freedom also remains elusive in states farther north, where she is continually on the lookout for slave patrollers, who had the power "to knock on anyone's door to pursue an accusation and for random inspections as well, in the name of public safety."

Such passages resonate today, given the shocking number of police killings of unarmed black men and boys, stepped-up ICE raids on immigrants, stop-and-frisk policies that target minorities, and President Trump's racist language that is empowering white supremacists. Whitehead does not accentuate such parallels. He does not need to. The excruciating tale he recounts here is the backstory to the injustices African Americans and immigrants continue to suffer, but a backstory only in the sense, as Faulkner put it, that "the past is never dead. It's not even past."

THE WORLD OF YESTERDAY

(1942; English translation, 1943)

Stefan Zweig
Translated by Benjamin W. Huebsch and Helmut Ripperger

The Austrian writer Stefan Zweig's memoir, *The World of Yesterday,* is an elegy for the lost world of his youth in fin de siècle Vienna. It's also an unnerving account of the horrors visited upon Europe during World War I, followed, after only a brief interlude of peace, by the cataclysmic rise of Hitler and the Continent's descent into World War II.

More than three-quarters of a century after it was published, his book reads as a haunting warning about the fragility of civilization and how quickly "the rule of raison" can give way to "the wildest triumph of brutality." It's a cautionary tale that could not be timelier today, given the weakening of the postwar liberal democratic order, in the face of an alarming resurgence of nationalism and far-right politics in Europe and the United States.

The worlds Zweig knew as a boy and later as a successful author during the era of the Weimar Republic will doubtless strike a chord with many readers in the opening decades of the twenty-first century. He wrote about growing up in a place and time when the miracles of science—the conquest of diseases, "the transmission of the human word in a second around the globe"—made progress seem inevitable, and even dire problems like poverty "no longer seemed insurmountable."